Channel Management

Patrick Forsyth

- ■ *The* fast track route to effective channel management

- ■ Covers key channel management techniques, from deciding the mix and ensuring customer focus to monitoring performance and channel innovation

- ■ Examples and lessons from benchmark companies, including Sharp and Sanwa and ideas from the smartest thinkers

- ■ Includes a glossary of key concepts and a comprehensive resources guide

>>EXPRESS EXEC.COM<<
essential management thinking at your fingertips

Copyright © Capstone Publishing 2002

The right of Patrick Forsyth to be identified as the author of this work has been asserted in accordance with the Copyright, Designs and Patents Act 1988

First published 2002 by
Capstone Publishing (A Wiley Company)
8 Newtec Place
Magdalen Road
Oxford OX4 1RE
United Kingdom
http://www.capstoneideas.com

CIP catalogue records for this book are available from the British Library and the US Library of Congress

ISBN 1-84112-195-9

Printed and bound in Great Britain

This book is printed on acid-free paper

Substantial discounts on bulk quantities of Capstone books are available to corporations, professional associations and other organizations. Please contact Capstone for more details on +44 (0)1865 798 623 or (fax) +44 (0)1865 240 941 or (e-mail) info@wiley-capstone.co.uk

Contents

Introduction to ExpressExec

ExpressExec is 3 million words of the latest management thinking compiled into 10 modules. Each module contains 10 individual titles forming a comprehensive resource of current business practice written by leading practitioners in their field. From brand management to balanced scorecard, ExpressExec enables you to grasp the key concepts behind each subject and implement the theory immediately. Each of the 100 titles is available in print and electronic formats.

Through the ExpressExec.com Website you will discover that you can access the complete resource in a number of ways:

» printed books or e-books;
» e-content – PDF or XML (for licensed syndication) adding value to an intranet or Internet site;
» a corporate e-learning/knowledge management solution providing a cost-effective platform for developing skills and sharing knowledge within an organization;
» bespoke delivery – tailored solutions to solve your need.

Why not visit www.expressexec.com and register for free key management briefings, a monthly newsletter and interactive skills checklists. Share your ideas about ExpressExec and your thoughts about business today.

Please contact elound@wiley-capstone.co.uk for more information.

Introduction

» Options for action
» A changing world

"In too many companies, the customer has become a bloody nuisance whose unpredictable behavior damages carefully made strategic plans, whose activities mess up computer operations, and who stubbornly insists that purchased products should work."
Lewis H Young, Editor-in-chief Business Week

Business has a complex job to do, and it is perfectly possible to get so bound up in the processes of running the organization that the external things – even customers, as highlighted above – are neglected. The area of distribution, and of selecting and managing channels of distribution, is one that needs an inherently externally focused view. Simplistically, distribution is just the link between an organization and its markets, but it is a complex process and one that offers many different options as a basis for how business activity is conducted.

OPTIONS FOR ACTION

Even a brief example illustrates this. If you are reading this work in book form, where was it bought? There is a whole list of possible sources, but consider just two: a large bookshop and an e-tailer (like Amazon or The Good Book Guide). Both are different shopping experiences for the reader, and both necessitate very different processes on the part of the publisher to ensure that the book is there for sale in each.

The bookshop is a traditional outlet. If it is a large one, a member of a chain perhaps, buying may take place centrally. Its buyers will deal with many different publishers and each must recognize and meet their expectations as to how that contact should be made with them. On the other hand an organization like Amazon did not even exist a few short years ago, but has become a major player in the book market with its own particular set of criteria and processes for purchase. A publisher has to relate well to each if they are to sell successfully. In addition, they have to consider a range of other outlets and chains of distribution that operate in the publishing area, from university outlets to party plan selling (the technique that is best known with organizations such as Tupperware).

Any organization must create suitable connections with the outside world and specifically with customers (using the term here to include all categories of customer, for example, the bookshop and the reader who shops there). This should not be an automatic process, one of just linking into the chain by hooking onto existing links, as it were. It is a creative process. Options have to be identified, choices have to be made about methods to be used, and not used. In all likelihood a mix of methods needs to be selected. The working processes to allow a channel to work effectively need to be set up, and the job of maintaining it and maximizing the way in which it serves the organization is an ongoing one.

A CHANGING WORLD

Nor is it a question of finding one solution that can then be regarded as fixed. Historically distribution may not have been regarded as a variable in quite the same way in which promotion was, for instance. Today, however, it is very much a variable. New methods of distribution are appearing, old ones are disappearing – and everything is changing. For many organizations another dimension here is the increasingly international nature of business. Distribution channels may well be complicated in a home market, if operations span the globe this complexity will increase.

Given this volatility, it is an area that needs regular review. And it is an area of *opportunity* – those who make their chosen channels of distribution work hardest for them are most likely to succeed.

Finally, as with so much else in marketing, the final arbiter here is the customer. If they do not like the product they will not buy it (or will not buy it again if, bought once, it proves a disappointment). If they do not like the way it is offered to them, because it is inconvenient, slow, uncertain or whatever, then they will not buy it, particularly if – as is so often the case – there are plenty of alternative suppliers waiting to be tried, who operate differently.

So channel management is potentially a significant element in the marketing armory. It is a significant part of an organization's relationship with their customers. We are all familiar with the thought that no man is an island. Similarly, no organization can operate without links to their market, and in today's competitive economy they must be good ones.

What is Channel Management?

- » The way to market
- » Channel management explained
- » The nature of successful channels
- » Summary

"When you boil it all down, your customers and clients use three criteria to measure you: communication, service and added value. How well you handle these three items is a reliable indicator of how long you'll keep your clients."

Mark McCormack, American sports marketing consultant and
author

Of all the management disciplines marketing is perhaps the most profligate with jargon and the least precise with much of its terminology. Distribution and channel management are a case in point. They are close relations and to clarify the picture we will look first at distribution.

THE WAY TO MARKET

Marketing must link to the market, not just in terms of having a focus on customers and their needs, but literally. Goods and services have to be taken to market and direct contact created with buyers. Distribution is the process that allows this to happen.

Let us take general principles first. However good any product or service, however well promoted and however much customers – and potential customers – want it, it has to be put in a position that gives people easy access to it; it must be distributed. And this can be a complex business, though it is certainly a marketing variable, albeit one that many regard as rather more fixed than in fact, it is. Consider the variety of ways in which goods are made available. Consumer products are sold in shops – retailers – but such may vary enormously in nature, from supermarkets and department stores, to specialist retailers, general stores and more – even market traders. These may, in turn, be variously located: in a town or city center, in an out of town shopping area, in a multi-story shopping center, or on a neighborhood corner site.

But the complexity does not stop there, retailers may be supplied by a network of wholesalers or distributors, or they may be simply not involved; some consumer products are sold by mail order, or door to door, or through home parties (like Tupperware). A similar situation applies to services; even traditional banking services being made available in stores, from machines in the street and through post and telephone – even on a drive-in basis. Banking is also an example of the changes going on in the area of distribution, many of these developments being comparatively recent moves away from solely traditional branch operations. Business to business, industrial products are similarly complex in the range of distributive options they use.

Areas where change has occurred, or is occurring, can prompt rapid customer reaction if whatever new means are offered prove to be convenient. Old habits may die hard, but if change is made attractive and visible then new practices can be established, and these too can then quickly become the norm. Conversely, if distribution method is inconvenient for customers then they will seek other ways of access to the product (or simply not buy it). Sometimes though, inconveniences are tolerated because need is high or compensated for by other factors. For example, there are some customers who will put up with queues in one shop only because the alternative is too far away, or has nowhere convenient to park.

New channels of distribution now exist as a result of the information technology revolution and the advent of various forms of e-commerce (see Chapter 4).

Similar *chains of distribution* exist in the marketing of every kind of product. The terminology may be a little different, distributors rather than retailers in industrial marketing, but the principles are essentially the same (see Fig. 2.1).

TYPES OF CHANNEL

Any such example is simplistic, the various possible types of entity involved and the chains down which things flow can vary considerably; as can the complexities involved.

So, let us be clear:

» *distribution* is the overall umbrella term encompassing the whole process;
» *chains of distribution* are the "routes" along which products "flow," as described above, to the ultimate consumer;
» *channels* is another word for chains, and is preferred in discussing the management processes involved; and
» *channel management* is thus the process of managing the distribution of products and services.

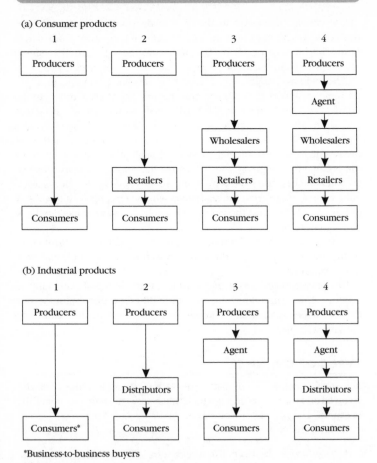

(a) Consumer products

(b) Industrial products

*Business-to-business buyers

Fig. 2.1 Chains of distribution.

More formally, the *Oxford Dictionary of Business* defines a distribution channel as "The network of firms necessary to distribute goods or services from the manufacturers to the consumers, the channel therefore consists of manufacturers, distributors, wholesalers and retailers."

CHANNEL MANAGEMENT EXPLAINED

Even at this level of detail it should now be apparent that distribution is crucial to marketing success; clearly products must be accessible to customers and, however well advertised they are, this is a prerequisite of their being purchased, at least in any quantity.

But distribution is more than just setting up a mechanism to make goods available. It also acts as part of the process that persuades people to buy. In other words, the quality of distribution – how well the various channels work – is a marketing variable. Managing the distribution process is a creative marketing activity which is conceptually no different from implementing a creative advertising campaign. There are several separate, but linked, aspects to channel management.

» *Channel choice*: decisions must be made about which channels will be used (and which will not). Note that channels are not mutually exclusive, several may be utilized together and the mix (and relative importance of different channels) is what must be fixed on. In addition, this is not choice as it were from a shopping list. Some channels are common, and utilized in a standard form. More often management is involved in creating a unique interpretation of what is done – their version of the utilization of that channel – and, sometimes, in creating new approaches entirely. The criteria for choice are investigated in Chapter 7.
» *Directing marketing activity towards different channels*: different channels involve accessing customers in different ways and may need different approaches and techniques. The sales element is often important here. For example, one channel may contain customers who can be handled successfully by the field force, another may demand a more sophisticated approach using key account managers.
» *Managing the channel at unit level*: if the channel consists in part of individual elements – for example some sort of distributor (organizations buying in something for subsequent resale, say) – then an individual relationship needs to be created between the parties. The organization must prompt them to do the best possible job on their behalf: this may involve everything from the provision of information to motivation and incentives for those involved.

THE NATURE OF SUCCESSFUL CHANNELS

The success of the way a channel operates, and how its distributive activity works for a particular product or organization is dependent on a number of factors: six are key.

» *Customer characteristics*: distributors are generally required when customers are widely dispersed, there are a large number of them and they buy frequently in small amounts. This is certainly true of many sectors of everyday product, less so or not at all with regard to more specialist items. Additionally, of course, customer preference is a vital factor. How do people *want* to buy things? What do they find most convenient and most enjoyable? This is especially important when new methods are considered (electronic issues again).

» *Product characteristics*: direct distribution is required when bulky or heavy products are involved. Bulky products need channel arrangements that minimize the shipping distance and the number of handlings; even a cursory look at physical distribution costs shows the importance of this factor. Where high unit value can cover higher unit selling costs, then any manufacturer can keep control over distribution by dealing direct; as with certain off the page distribution systems, or at the far end of the spectrum, the likes of those who sell door-to-door. Finally, products requiring installation or maintenance are generally sold through a limited network, such as sole agents, so that such factors can more easily be controlled.

» *Distributor characteristics*: distributors are more useful when their skills of low cost contact, service and storage are more important than their lack of commitment to one product or brand. If very specific support is necessary then other options may be preferred.

» *Competitive characteristics*: the channels chosen may often be influenced by the channels competitors use, and there may be dangers in moving away too far and too fast from what a market expects and likes. The competitive interaction in this way between retailers is another variable. In the area of fast food, Burger King try to obtain sites near to McDonald's. On the other hand, some manufacturers, such as Avon Cosmetics, choose not to compete for scarce positions in retail stores and have established profitable door-to-door direct selling operations instead. Similarly, major chains may seek to open branches near existing smaller, independent, retailers, not only to take advantage of their market knowledge – they are in an area where there is a demand – but with the aim of replacing them altogether. This last may well not be entirely in customers' interests and illustrates one aspect of the sheer power wielded by major retailing groups.

» *Company characteristics*: the size of a company often correlates with its market share. The bigger its market share, the easier it is to find distributors willing to handle the product – thus even a small shop is likely to find a corner for major brands, and will be selective about what else they stock. They may not be able to stock everything, but will find space for anything they believe in. Where there is clearly profit to be made no one wants to miss out on it.

Similarly, a supplier may be innovative (and/or build on a strength) and seek ways of becoming less dependent on the normal chain of distribution. Creativity may have a role to play here. For instance, cosmetics may sell well in outlets that simply display them, but some stores putting on make-up demonstrations (or letting the manufacturer do so) may create an edge; for a while. Additionally, a policy of fast delivery is less compatible with a large number of stages in the channel and there is a danger that slow delivery (measured in market terms) dilutes marketing effectiveness. As service standards increase so there is less room for anyone that lags behind to do as well as they might – increasingly slow delivery is not something customers are prepared to accept.

» *Environmental characteristics*: changes in the economic and legal environment can also bring about changes in distributive structures. For example, when the market is depressed, manufacturers want to move their goods to market in the most economic way. They thus cut out intermediaries or unessential services, to allow them to compete on price and deal direct. Again, legal restrictions have been introduced in the UK in recent years to prevent channel character-istics that may weaken competition (e.g. the recent prohibition on manufacturers dictating price in the medicines market).

How a company analyses the distributive possibilities and organizes to utilize a chosen method or methods effectively is certainly important to overall marketing success. It is affected too by any overall trend in the market place. For example, if out of town shopping centers are thriving it may make sense to use them; or not.

Success is also in the details, everything from the strategic view taken of channel management to the tactics of working through a particular individual distributor perhaps.

SUMMARY

The elements conditioning this area of marketing are complex and interlocking, one thing affects another and, at the end of the day, it is the overall mix that matters and how it is managed. The key issues are to:

» make good channel choice decisions and never regard them as fixed for ever;
» create strategic marketing approaches that make sense for each channel;
» manage the relationships involved, especially where success is dependent on other people along the chain over whom no direct control is possible; and
» focus throughout the process on the customer, no scheme and no channel will bring commercial success unless it is satisfactory in consumer terms; and ideally, of course, customers must find that it meets their needs and is entirely to their tastes.

The Evolution of Channel Management

''A day in the life of a consumer in the 1990s is very different to what it was in the 1980s. Change is visible everywhere. Drive down any highway, visit a shopping mall, or turn on the television and we see a whole range of options for buying products that were just emerging or did not exist a few years ago.''

B. Rosenbloom, author Marketing Channels: A Management View

Products and services have always needed a route to market. Distribution overall, and channels of distribution in particular, are thus an original part of the earliest commercial transactions. We have records of retail shops in simple form thousands of years ago and can imagine similar in stone-age caves. Today the complexities of distribution, and the varied nature of the channels and kinds of organization that is involved are legion.

Here we examine the main influences that, in recent years and back, say 30/40 years, have created the picture we see today.

CHANGE EQUALS OPPORTUNITY

Let us be clear at the start. Growing complexity and specialization in this area provide opportunities for everyone in marketing. Marketing must view everything about distribution as a variable. How, exactly how, the mix of options is organized by any individual supplier provides an opportunity to maximize their effectiveness in the market place. Furthermore it is an opportunity to differentiate, in other words decisions made about such factors can create an edge against competitors. Distribution used to be viewed by many people as something pretty well fixed, now it must be worked with in the same way as any other marketing variable – and is instrumental, albeit amongst other factors, in dictating what success is enjoyed in the market place.

Several general trends have changed things over the years.

Size does matter

The first is the question of size of customer. It may be most obvious in retail operations, but is essentially similar in most industries – customers, or many of them, have got larger and that makes them change in nature and contact with them may well need different handling.

As an example, in publishing (where the author began his career in the sixties) the UK retail market was dominated by one major retailer, WH Smith. They were seen as being very important and they were demanding too, with relationships between their central organization and branches (individual shops) being important to co-ordinate. The next largest, for example John Menzies, were not on the same scale and a very significant part of the market was the independent bookshops. Today it makes a good example of change, the retail book market is dominated by large chains: these include Waterstone's, Books etc. (recently bought by the American group Borders), Ottakers and more, alongside WH Smith and John Menzies who continue to operate, though books are a small part of their product range.

Small book shops are fewer on the ground and several book e-tailers, like Amazon, have added to the changing picture. Retailers like supermarkets, who years ago stocked no books, have become significant outlets at least for some books. To reinforce the point by reference to another sector it is worth noting that in the last forty years two thirds of the independent retailers in the grocery business have closed.

With increasing size have come other changes. Any major group, whether a retail chain or anything else, exhibits various characteristics that all affect their suppliers, such as the following.

» *Buying power*: size gives large customers the power to be demanding. This may mean that larger discounts are given, margins eroded and that the smaller players find it even more difficult to compete. It can also mean that there is pressure to supply many other kinds of support: special delivery arrangements, special packing, promotional support, extended credit terms etc. In many markets the penalty of losing business with a major player is huge (for example, in the UK five retail groups account for almost all the goods sold of a "supermarket" nature – miss out on one and a supplier loses a significant part of the total market). Thus the pressure on suppliers is considerable. There has been a steady trend for the big to get bigger, perhaps from the mid 1970s on, and the trend continues.

» *Professionalism*: alongside the trend above, the individual buyers have become more skillful. If you want to know about the skill of negotiation or numeracy – ask a professional buyer. In terms of the skills necessary to do the job, expertise was boosted by intensive training, particularly in the late 1970s and 1980s. Now the people involved are almost always a force to be reckoned with.

» *Systems*: alongside both the above, more recent developments have given retailers a further edge. Information technology has provided new and enhanced abilities to collect and manipulate data that assists organizing to achieve maximization of profitability. More of this in Chapter 4.

Alongside this – the complexity mounts – the initiatives taken regarding methods of distribution have expanded the options for consumers and thus for those who supply goods through chains of this sort.

Keeping control

The response of some to a changing distributive scene has been to avoid it, or rather to avoid multi-layered approaches, keeping direct control and dealing as directly as possible. Examples include:

» specialist publishers (like Usborne who sell children's books through party plan (Tupperware-style));
» business book publishers (like Gower Publishing) who channel most of their activity directly to individual buyers by using direct mail;
» banks and insurance companies that deal direct from telephone call centers;
» banks and others (including a growing number of travel companies) whose only link with customers is via the internet; and
» companies (like Bodyshop) who sell only through their own retail outlets.

Of course, in such examples various methods may be used – a mix is nearly always involved.

A plethora of options

The following all have comparatively short histories. Such a list shows the dynamic nature of channels and how both new methods are originated and older ones evolve.

» Direct supply, as for instance with catalogues, has increased and spread, with a company like clothe's supplier Land's End operating exclusively this way on an international basis, as do Dell in the very different arena of computer sales.

» Stores have grown, changed or specialized. As the large ones sell a wider range and stay open longer, others have narrowed what they sell in some cases dramatically (e.g. Tie Rack).

» Specialist outlets have diversified so much that they are effectively different entities; for example petrol stations have not only added shops selling things for the motorist, they stock heavy things best picked up by car (e.g. potatoes), while others have targeted petrol sale sites to offer a fuller range (e.g. Tesco Metro).

» Stores have gone out of town and so-called retail parks are now a significant part of the shopping landscape.

» Factory outlets (like Freeport in Essex) are more in evidence.

» Call centers expand into more and more areas of purchase.

» Shops within shops are a common element of many large stores.

» On-line shopping remains difficult to predict but in some form seems to be here to stay.

» Own brands have almost the same credibility as any other; and more than some.

» Retailers have become global brands, for example UK Tesco grocery supermarkets trading successfully under their home name in markets as different as Thailand, and Japanese department store operator Isetan is opening in Europe.

» Catalogue stores (or warehouses?), like Argos, compete successfully with more conventional stores offering much higher levels of service.

The list could be extended and will no doubt continue to grow. At the same time a wealth of small, often specialist outlets continue to find favor with the public and take their share of total sales. You can buy food direct from the farm (and pick your own strawberries), shop (from the National Trust) as you visit a stately home, buy whisky on board an airliner, have your lunchtime sandwiches delivered to your office and ... but the list is near endless. In recent years the move from shopping being a chore to the concept of shopping as entertainment – the "shopping experience" – creates an appetite amongst customers for new ways of doing things.

Or the customer can be drawn into the process and sales can find other ways of bypassing more conventional routes, as Avon do with cosmetics and toiletries.

Everywhere there is innovation, and creative ideas about how opportunities can be created for customers to buy and buy more. Even some unlikely businesses seem to make progress and change things. McDonalds may not provide your favorite food, but they are seemingly everywhere. Their outlets initially stayed very much the same as they expanded massively internationally. Then they added drive-ins, and started to seek new places to locate, with airports being one successful addition. Now, the nature of the outlet itself is changing. Mini-outlets in kiosk form are appearing. In Singapore there are two apparently thriving no more than a hundred meters apart, and within easy walking distance of a normal outlet.

Accessibility

Another important change of recent years in the retail area is that of opening hours. More than 5 million people in the UK now regard their main shopping time as being after 10 pm and a whole variety of changes have occurred here, for instance:

» late opening (and in some cases 24 hour opening) is now common;
» flexible hours are much used, for example varying on different days of the week;
» the traditional British "half day closing" day of the week is now almost totally gone;
» Sunday opening is now almost universal (even the UK department store group John Lewis, for long holding out against this, announced changes as this was being written – a step in the open direction); and
» call centers in industries like travel and banking have long hours during which they can be contacted.

At the same time, in other industries, any special factors affecting hours need to be respected. For example, it is usual in plant hire for companies to start early so that if a machine is found not to be working as work starts on a building site, customers can make contact and arrange to hire a replacement with no delay to work.

Service

There is a strong link between distribution and service. For example, as supermarkets have taken a greater and greater share of the food market, independent retailers have kept a healthy business in particular areas with many people prepared to pay a premium for "proper bread" say. The service element generally amongst small operators has become more important as competitors have got larger, and perhaps more impersonal. There is a strong link here between all this and segmentation and niche marketing.

Battle of the brands

A major trend to watch is the way that major brands are lined up against some major outlets, as currently are Levis jeans and Tesco in the UK. Levis takes the view that where their brand is sold is key to its image and thus success. They want their products sold primarily in quality, upmarket outlets where they will command the premium price. This creates their ability to spend on marketing in a way that created the quality and life-style image in the first place, and also acts to maintain and enhance it. They do not want to see their product piled high and cheap in what they regard as the wrong kind of outlet.

Simple. If a manufacturer does not like an outlet they do not sell to them and that is an end to the matter. No. It is not that simple and the reason is the complex nature of distribution and the various channels and outlets it involves. So, as a result retailers unable to deal direct can often find a wholesaler, distributor or some entity from whom they can buy so called "gray" products (and if from overseas gray imports).

Currently legal battles are on the go or pending. Certain retailers are crying "restrictive practice," and manufacturers like Levis (it seems to affect fashion products especially) are claiming their right to trade as they wish and that this is in the customers' long term interests. The jury is out, but changes are doubtless on the way.

The industrial dimension

Although most emphasis here has been put on consumer goods marketing, industrial and business to business marketing has been subject to similar changes. Such do not show in the high street, of course, but many of the trends are there. A business may buy its computers on line or over the telephone (e.g. from Dell), bank in a way that has no physical branch (i.e. by telephone, post or internet), and book their business travel on line rather than going to a conventional corporate travel agent. Industrial products are sold through a whole gamut of intermediaries such as wholesalers, distributors, dealers and agents and there are almost as many permutations regarding how things can be organized here as in the more visible, consumer product areas.

Even small ideas to change the way customers relate to you can be useful. For example, an office equipment firm now opens on Saturdays, making its town center car park available for people going into town to shop. This is linked to a promotion that invites people to attend demonstrations while their families are at the shops. For families that are organized that way, it works too; yet not so long ago they were firmly closed at weekends "like our business customers."

WHERE NEXT?

The overall feeling here is one of change. One thing leads to another and there is both a degree of "me-too-ism" about the take up of changes, and an opportunity to innovate. So, it matters less who started say a move to late or Sunday opening amongst retailers, but once started it tends to spread. The mix of ideas that are used by any organization will be, in part, copied and, should also be, partly innovative.

Not that new developments are entirely positive in their effect. Consider late opening again. It may increase costs, complicate staffing and, in the end, only spread the same amount of business over a longer period of time. But one organization doing it may win out, so others have to follow. As the end result is never the final word and will never remove all problems – the search for new methods, large and small goes on.

Ultimately the evolution of distribution and the channels and methods it involves must be customer focused. This is a prime consideration in all decisions in this area – see Chapter 6, and certainly initiatives stand or fall on how well customers like them. If no one wants to buy stocks and shares in their pajamas at three in the morning then providing such a facility will just cost money to no advantage. If a particular method of purchase is made possible and rings bells with customers, then it can also provide an edge in the market place – for a while at least.

SUMMARY

The history of distributive practice shows clearly that:

» distribution methods and channels are changing and a variety of influences make continuing change likely too;
» it pays to watch for trends and changes, and perhaps to aim to keep ahead of them, certainly to keep abreast of them;
» this is an area where change often indicates opportunity; and
» that whatever changes occur their lasting is dependent on customer preference.

The E-Dimension

- » Communication
- » Computer systems
- » The effectiveness of channels
- » New channels
- » A clash of channels
- » Best practice
- » Right here and now
- » Summary

"To warrant serious pursuit, an idea must be both practical and useful. Out of those ideas that are practical, a smaller number may be useful. To be useful, an invention must not only fill a need, it must be an economical and efficient solution to that need."

David Packard, joint founder of Hewlett Packard

Some things have become routine as technology has brought an electronic element to bear on so much. For instance, industrial customers are used to seeing sales people with laptop computers (and certain consumer products utilize this too, for example in financial services). Their use can bring an immediate rise in service levels to the relationship between many suppliers and their customers. However, it is axiomatic in addressing the topic here that this section will be out of date before you can read it. This fact makes a powerful first point: everything in the area of information technology is changing very fast. What is happening is potentially very powerful. Richard Ingleton, corporate development director for KPMG, was quoted recently in the journal *Marketing Business* as saying, "A year ago, there was a healthy skepticism around e-business and what it meant. Now there is recognition that a huge amount can be gained from optimizing existing businesses through e-business."

One of the prime areas where there is impact is in what has been traditionally called distribution, and thus on channel effectiveness and channel management. The scale of the e-changes is broad. Richard Ingleton adds: "Remember this isn't about technology. Technology may be the enabler, but it's not the answer. It's as much about process and change management as it is about which bit of technology we use."

That said, we can usefully look at those areas of channel management where an effect is in train, albeit resisting the temptation to offer too much by way of prediction. There are several overall areas to look at:

COMMUNICATION

A major area of impact for information technology is with communications. Indeed much is only a changed form of communication. But the changes may be significant.

» *e-mail* can speed communication, helpful everywhere and especially so with far flung overseas distributors. It is different from other forms of communication too, for instance being more informal (and therefore less appropriate at least for some customer communications).

» *Web sites* are, certainly at their simplest, only a new form of communication, an electronic brochure perhaps. They can also become far more: a means of selling as well as promoting and thus a new distributive channel, as well as serving other purposes such as facilitating research. It should be noted that there are a great many very poor web sites about, a sign perhaps of the stage two to four years back when the only objective of many was "to have one, and quick." To get even a simple one right needs care, and the process of ensuring it remains right is ongoing. Much advice and assistance is available for those who want it (see box) and it is an area to go into with eyes wide open and with due consideration.

THE SECRETS OF E-SUCCESS

1 Give your customers what they want: first be clear about your target (it may be difficult to be all things to all people), find out – through research – what they really want and aim for every entry in a web site to work effectively.

2 Create an intelligent exchange: find out the process visitors are engaged in (e.g. solving a problem, answering a question) and make the site help them through that process.

3 Design and interface is as important as functionality: in other words recognize how short a time you have to hook people, interest them fast and make staying with you attractive and easy.

4 Brand and promotion is key: you cannot rely on people simply beating a path to your web site (or on search engines leading them there) you have to actively generate traffic.

5 Test market: do not rush, test that a significant number of key contacts like what you are doing (in all its detail) before you go live.

6 Develop your experiential marketing skills: you have to have the skills these new methods demand: such include proficiency

with the technology and a range of appropriate marketing skills (e.g. customer behavior analysis).

7 Recognize that the process is in its infancy: you need to progress surely and deal with a situation where many aspects of the process will change and move ahead as you do so.

These key points are essentially those propounded by one specialist in this area (Pauline Bickerton. Managing Director of consultants MarketingNet). They certainly encapsulate the key issues here and provide a basis for producing a more tailored version ahead of action in your own organization.

COMPUTER SYSTEMS

Computers seem to become obsolete faster and faster. Not all that is added and that changes is useful, but there are key areas here which relate to channel management and the sophistication grows; certainly a constant eye needs to be kept on what will in future be possible and how it will help. Meantime, the following are good examples of current capabilities (and will doubtless themselves increase in sophistication).

» *Analysis*: a variety of systems and software is now available to help analysis and thus decision making and action. More can be tailored to individual requirements and this becomes more economic as time goes by. A classic case here is to put the equivalent of a "market map" (see Chapter 8) into a form so that a computer can be used to provide an up to date picture of the revenue and profit flowing through different channels. Such information can provide a sound basis for review and decision making, and literally act as an aid to fine tuning the strategy for channels.

» Systems: the best example here is that of customer relationship management (CRM). This is an umbrella term for systems that range from an automated customer-contact system to assist the sales force, to an all embracing, organization-wide culture that pools information from different departments to ensure a co-ordinated overall approach to customer and account management. Whatever channels are used, such systems can be made specific to the contacts necessary along a particular chain. It is vital that such systems are not adopted in generic form and that activity stems from them regardless of need. They should respect the individual nature of an organization's customers and be used to provide a route map to effective operations, not a straitjacket that curbs flexibility and reduces service levels.

As an example of a particular activity that helps one particular system I would mention merchandising. Suppliers selling through retailers benefit from good merchandising. They may help with what is done to increase its effect on their product. One area that computers can now make precise is the vexed question of what goes where. A program can look at a list of variables such as product size, price, margin and rate of turnover and work out the optimum arrangement for a given shelf area in order to maximize sales. By avoiding gaps (because of awkward pack sizes) and getting the right amount of different products from a range sales are helped. This was a technique pioneered by Fisher Price for their range of toys, but can be used in many different product areas. Such a system clearly helps the efficiency of how a channel works and is good for relationships between supplier and retailer also.

THE EFFECTIVENESS OF CHANNELS

Choices about which channels should be used and how they should be managed are constantly being affected by the march of technology at channel level. There is too much happening here to give more than an example or two, but how advantage is taken of such situations is an important consideration in organizing overall marketing strategy. An ongoing watching brief needs to be kept on developments, some element of prediction brought to bear and marketing action plans adapted to accommodate the new situation in a positive way.

» *Supermarket example*: the sophistication here is considerable, particularly in the way information about individual customers can be gathered and used. Electronic tills, credit and store cards all link to provide detailed information about customers' likes and dislikes and their behavior. As a card is zapped at the cash point, already computers can link into a customer's previous buying history: what brand of coffee do they buy? What promotions does it make sense to give them in light of that? This whole area continues to change rapidly.

» *Call center*: here is a channel that makes good use of technology. Just asking for a post code can put a customer's full address on screen as a call is taken, and allow contact to be handled in light of any previous contact they have had with the organization in the past, details of which are also shown. The link here between technology and the standard of service customers perceive as they do business in this way (along this channel) is clear.

NEW CHANNELS

Perhaps the most difficult area on which to comment in light of how it is changing is e-commerce itself. It takes many forms, of course, and encompasses an organization adding a web site to their marketing armory and equipping it with a facility for people to place orders on it, to fully fledged e-tailers selling a range of products just like a store of some sort. All these constitute examples of a channel that did not exist a few short years ago.

E-tailers may mirror the retail scene. There are shops that sell one product, a closely allied range or more. There are e-shops that are independent businesses and others that are the e-arm of an existing business; thus books can be bought from Amazon, or from Barnes and Noble or Waterstone's. Other examples have little or no relationship with retail; other than providing new forms of competition. One such is Napster. After long battles about their free provision for downloading M-3 format music off the web, they have now forged an agreement with the music industry and will charge a fee. Buying tracks of music sitting at your desk seems to have become a formal (and respectable?) channel amongst the more traditional ways.

E-tailing, despite some failures and uncertainties, seems to be here to stay. The list of products sold this way is steadily increasing and has moved a long way from the CD, books and videos that predominated in the early days. A new electronic distribution channel is now available to be part of anyone's mix; it will no doubt grow and evolve as time passes. Just how exactly, remains to be seen. One example of an area that remains unclear is Internet selling by supermarkets. Some customers find the idea unattractive (or frightening?), others find it tedious to order so many different items – though repeat purchases make it easier. Others confidently predict the demise of the supermarket. They see a future where all commodity type products – everything from cat food to detergent – will be ordered electronically and delivered. Shops, smaller than today's supermarkets will consist largely of departments like meat, cheese and others that need real choice. We will see.

A CLASH OF CHANNELS

One thing is worth pondering in any prediction you may care to make and that is the relationship, at customer level, of e-tailers and more conventional outlets.

Some things can work fine exclusively through Internet channels. If someone wants to buy a new novel by a favorite author, they are probably happy not even to look at it – they tap into *amazon.com* or whoever, call up the title and place their order (with maybe a little price comparison along the way). Other purchases are more complex. If someone wants a new CD player, say, they may well want to look at it – better still to hear it and check it out. They go to a retailer and do just that. Then they might elect to visit a number of sites on the Internet, compare prices, check delivery and so on and place an order. What many people will not do is simply order a machine seen only on a monitor screen.

In other words retailing is currently necessary for certain kinds of e-commerce to work. Other sites exist to help the process of choice, providing a comprehensive list of the prices for which a particular product is selling, at a specific moment, in a variety of outlets.

How this clash works out and what future buying practice will be like is still uncertain. That said e-commerce works well for many things, the fields in which it operates are growing and more and more people are either experimenting with this sort of shopping or expressing confidence in it and becoming regulars. One of the most important things is, unsurprisingly, service. Customers want advice, they want to be able to change things and they want to be able to make contact easily and get any problem sorted out. In this area too, after initial uncertainties, things seem to be getting better. Maybe in the future e-retailing will be the predominant channel of distribution for many things. Again we will see.

BEST PRACTICE

To conclude this section two very different examples of success are mentioned.

» *Checking the state of the art*: first, anyone aiming to directly use e-retailing as a channel along which their organization can trade should look at what is being done by others and recognize that implementing anything that falls much short of the best is wasted effort. Of course you do not have to copy slavishly, and you will no doubt want to add ideas of your own and amend things you see in operation elsewhere.

So, look at some of your own favorites – I would suggest Amazon in all its international forms – and see how they operate. Particularly look at two things:

» how easy they are to navigate (customers' patience is limited – something that takes just a few seconds longer than they feel it should or are used to elsewhere may prompt their logging off); and

» how well they *sell* (such a site is not just an information source – it should speak to people and do persuasively).

Current practice, and what customers like, is certainly part of what your own solutions need to be based on. Technology needs to be used creatively here, but also kept in check. Just because something is technically possible does not mean customers will like it; at the end of the day, if cleverness and clarity (and ease of use) are in competition, then think very carefully before voting for anything other than clarity.

» *Boosting performance long distance*: another manifestation of information technology is e-learning (in all its forms). Many companies are using this as a major part of their overall development activity. One such is Reuters. David Cook, that organization's distance learning manager, was quoted recently in *Marketing Business* magazine as saying: "It's helping foster a 'learning culture' where staff integrate the use of web-based learning materials into their normal work patterns as performance support." He goes on to speak about staff receiving "timely training . . . delivered to their desks."

A clear application for such delivery is with the plethora of dealers and distributors that are part of many organizations' overseas channels of distribution. The people in them, from principal to sales staff, need support of various kinds. In part this will include: product information and advice (and techniques for selling the product represented successfully) – both areas that are expensive to deliver by sending out a trainer, especially if there are many territories to be contacted. E-learning is a real asset here, allowing a precise message to be passed on, in a context where real training takes place, and in a way that demonstrates commitment to the distributor as well as equipping them with skills that will help their business and that of those they represent.

Such innovation must not be allowed to dilute personal contact. People still need to visit distributors, but overall frequency – and usefulness – of contact can be increased if an appropriate mix of contacts and methods of contact is used. The effect of good, regular and constructive contact on the effectiveness of a distributor may make all the difference. What is wanted is not an organization "going through the motions" and then their distributor feeling the organization they represent takes them for granted. Rather the best outcome is one where the distributor provides excellent representation, not least because they are truly involved with their principal and feel – and are – supported in the job they do on their behalf.

Now a final example, that is nearer to home.

Right here and now

Obtaining and reading this work itself provides an example of new channel exploitation in action. As well as being available in book form through a range of channels (see the market map of publishing in Chapter 8), it is available, in sections, downloaded in electronic form. While electronic books to read on the beach with some sort of electronic viewer are still a way off, more and more is happening in this way. Certainly this is so in the publication of business material (another is the provision of material to be read on Palm-type handheld machines, something being done in the business area by Estuary Technology). The initiative currently being taken by Capstone Publishing with this *Express-Exec* series is a bold one. They will I hope forgive me for suggesting that by the time these words appear, or soon after, it could be regarded as routine and certainly something else will make the best example of current innovation!

SUMMARY

The electronic revolution presents a significant opportunity for getting the most from the channel management process. Its effect is diverse, but some things we can be clear about:

» constant review is necessary to keep up to date in this area;
» a willingness to experiment may be necessary; and
» solutions and action must be realistically based, not just technology driving on regardless or used just because it is there, but implementation based on what will work – and, not least, work for customers old and new.

The Global Dimension

"Anyone chasing the holy grail of an ad that will appeal to a Brit, a German and a Frenchman is a jerk."

Mike Moran, marketing director for Toyota (UK)

It is channels of distribution that take your goods to market. That market might be down the road or on the other side of the world. Many of the principles at work are similar in either case, but channels must relate closely to customers and they – and their likes, dislikes and preferences may vary around the globe.

RELATIVE SCALES OF BUSINESS

There is a plethora of examples of different scales of international operation. These range from a company based in one country and exporting to a few others, to a multinational organization whose name you see at any international airport you emerge from in any part of the world. It is no real surprise that the Coca Cola logo is quoted as being recognized by more people around the world than any other graphic image of any sort.

Global marketing is on the increase. Just looking at the visible retail sector alone, there is ample evidence of this increasing globalization. Tesco (UK) operates, under the Catteeau name, in France. Hennes & Mauritz (Sweden) is doing well in Germany, Wall-Mart (USA) proceeds largely by acquisition, most recently buying the German hypermarket chain Wertkauf. Many are moving into the old "eastern" bloc European countries, with Ahold (Holland) acquiring a dozen or so supermarkets in the Czech Republic, for example, and names like Toys R Us, Gap, IKEA and more are seen in more and more locations. A long list of different companies and different ways of expanding could be made.

Two broad categories of organization are worth noting.

1. Exporters

This term is used to describe the many permutations of doing business in another country essentially without setting up an operation there. The prime channels are therefore routes through local distributors and dealers chosen, not least for their local knowledge, but with a list of other criteria in mind (see Chapter 6). A broad difference is the range of products such distributors sell.

» They may be *exclusive*, that is they sell one product of a sort and the arrangement guarantees that they will not distribute competing products (though they may sell a range of non-competitive products).
» They may be the reverse of this, selling a whole range of similar products, effectively in competition with each other, but providing a different service to their customers.

In both cases communication and support is essential. Simplistically, exclusive dealers must feel they make enough from the arrangement or they may seek to substitute one product for another they regard as a better prospect to provide their profitability. For the supplier, if a range of competing products is sold, then constant contact is necessary, designed to encourage an emphasis of activity on the particular product in question.

For some, distribution overseas is a small, discrete, part of their operation. For others it is more significant. Some – our second category – think less of their home and overseas markets and operate more in terms of the world market.

2. International operators

Here again the scale may vary but the involvement is different. The principle is much more actively involved in the overseas operations. They may set up subsidiaries, joint companies, make franchise or licensing arrangements – or operate in a variety of other ways.

In either case any brand involved may form part of the arrangement; certainly this is usual with larger organizations and ''big'' brands (though sometimes names must be changed for particular local markets).

OUR WAY OR YOUR WAY?

Any degree of global marketing increases the scale on which channel selection and management of chosen channels must take place. Decisions may need to be made market by market. What is right for one country may not be for another. What is more, methods that are transferable, that is what has been worked out and works well at home, may – or may not – work well elsewhere. Whatever options are selected, channel management – active management to make sure all works well – is always necessary.

Some things do seem to work well in a variety of markets. Consider certain well-known companies.

» McDonalds franchise their burger restaurants and they look and operate in much the same way across most of the world, with minor differences in menu. But distribution methods and product acceptance are inextricably linked. For example, when McDonalds commenced business in South East Asia there was considerable local skepticism about whether the product was right for the local population. It was difficult to find anyone to take on a franchise, and finally the first shop opened in Singapore gave a very attractive deal to the local franchisee. But the locals quickly responded as elsewhere, indeed it became the company's single most profitable outlet in the world for a while (and the original owner is reputed to have become a millionaire several times over). The franchise system worked well here too as expansion continued.

» Bodyshop have outlets that appear very similar in many parts of the world, their preferred channel is to sell their own products through their own outlets.

Accepted ways of working in one country can not only work in others, they can change the whole local scene. Tesco are currently opening and operating supermarkets in Thailand, a country where the word supermarket conjures up visions of something of no great size at all. It is early days, but they are performing well and literally changing the shopping habits of thousands of local people. While the many small retailers adversely affected are not too pleased, others see the opportunity to supply Tesco, for instance with the local food products that they need, and are exploring the potential of this large new customer. Equally an organization may have to adopt local ways in local markets, and for many, the complexities of international working are compounded by the need to work in a variety of different ways across the markets with which they deal.

STRATEGY FOR SUCCESS

Cross border marketing and distribution seems to work best when it fulfils six criteria.

1 *A strong corporate philosophy*: in other words a strong brand image, corporate identity, style and culture – that travels.
2 *A genuinely new offering*: it may be radically different (like Tesco in Thailand) or more a matter of style, shopping experience or value, but it must exist – there is no right for every retail concept to work everywhere no matter how closely it mirrors existing practice.
3 *An appropriate format*: whether it is high-quality (like Gap), discounting (like Aldi), specialist sector focus (like Toys R Us), or high-end luxury (like brands such as Gucci or what the now troubled Marks and Spencer have done in Europe and Asia).
4 *A clear target market*: often younger rather than older, affluent rather than further down market seems most favored.
5 *Commitment*: such global expansion needs to have weight behind it: money and perhaps especially dedicated people at senior level.
6 *A long term view*: it may take time, expecting or insisting on a rapid return may kill a project stone dead (e.g. IKEA was in the States for eight years before it made a profit, yet their expansion has continued successfully).

NOTE: these criteria stem from research done by Deloitte & Touche Consulting, and to be complete one should probably add *product acceptability* to the list.

Certainly international business brings increased risk and a sound understanding of local markets (and therefore local knowledge) is important.

THE SERVICE DIMENSION

An important area for many products when operating at a distance is service. This may mean a customer having the ability to get parts and repairs done on something like a camera or a radio, and get it fast, easily and effectively – especially so if anything is necessary during a warranty period. Similarly with industrial products, though the problem of providing appropriate service for a piece of earth moving equipment while it is working half way up the mountains in, say, Peru is somewhat greater. Some companies major on service in the overall profile they project (Caterpillar Tractors is an example) – but whatever channel of distribution is chosen it must not only be suitable for providing market access, but must cope efficiently with this aspect too. Where distributors are used, their ability to provide an appropriate level of after sales and other service is a crucial criteria in selecting and appointing representatives.

KEEPING IN TOUCH

A major difference between home based operations and global ones for many organizations is simply the distances involved. A variety of types of organization may be involved, of course, but let us keep the classic overseas distributor in mind. Without a doubt the level, quality and frequency of contact maintained is a significant direct influence on the success of the relationship and the level of revenue produced.

Such contact must:

» *provide information* (sound, useful and timely);
» *be motivational* (to people ranging from the distributor's principal to their sales and service staff); and
» *genuinely help to improve business performance* (thus making the relationship work, promoting loyalty and helping increase sales).

The genuine help provided can involve a number of different things, including assistance for the distributor with:

» *Planning*
» *Finances and financing*
» *Training*
» *Staff maintenance and motivation*
» *Industry and competitive intelligence*
» *Technical innovation*
» *Public relations and image*
» *Standards and controls*
» *Business efficiency and improvement of effectiveness*.

All these are in addition to physical help (e.g. building, and perhaps paying for, a showroom), and they are all essentially matters of commu-nication. Providing support of this sort is a simple concept, but needs commitment to implement an ongoing communications strategy and program that will act to direct the distributor toward the principal's ends (though perhaps they are better regarded as joint ends). Modern communication methods should make elements of this easier than ever before, though how many managers have resolved to send an overseas colleague an e-mail to say *well done* for something, and somehow have yet to find time to write it? So, it needs working at but, when this is done, it can pay dividends.

For example, one North American company, which sells construction and similar equipment across the world, have for many years used one of these methods, that of training, to enhance both the relationship they have with their distributors and to equip them and their people to perform better on their behalf. In part the training is technical, that much is simply necessary, though they handle it to maximize its impact. But they also offer sales training, training in negotiating skills and financial management (and more) to boost the personal skills deployed by distributors' staff on their behalf to sell their product. Costs are subsidized, effectively shared therefore, and the investment is seen as a worthwhile element of the budget covering the costs of managing the overseas channel of distribution involved.

A WIRED WORLD

The IT revolution (see Chapter 4) has provided a new way to implement a global channel of distribution – without leaving your desk, as it were. E-tailing apart, large numbers of organizations now have Web sites; at the beginning of 2001 this ranged from 66% of UK companies, of which 57% allowed customers to order direct, to 59% in Germany and Sweden, 63% in USA and 55% in Canada. This may lead the way into international distribution, it may go in parallel with other channels, or provide a way of stimulating orders from a market where no other activity is undertaken, but almost certainly it complicates matters.

Setting up this sort of facility seems easy, but of course it must be done well. People must recognize the product and be aware of the route to information and purchase before they can, or will, act. Many people log onto sites and give up on them because they are confusing or badly organized. In addition, setting up the facility is one thing; leading people to it and prompting its use is quite another. Richard Thompson, CEO of Mosaic Technology, is quoted as saying "Global brands are becoming common in the local marketplace but the acceptance of brands on a global basis is not something that will happen overnight. After all, how can a brand be successful in a number of different countries or regions without direct and tactical knowledge of the local marketplace and the local consumer?'' So, while e-commerce provides seemingly instant access to the markets of the world all at once, the facts suggest that concentrating on supplying specific markets through their own local channels has merit too.

For a while these two approaches will doubtless coexist; thereafter who knows where we will go next?

BEST PRACTICE

A simple, well executed, example with which to end. One that illustrates the way in which a channel can be identified and focused upon, and how specific action can be taken to drive business through it.

Guinness make stout, which we might think of as both an acquired taste and a rather idiosyncratic product – very Irish. Yet they see their market as a broad one and operate in many countries – unexpectedly perhaps Malaysia is an enormous market where Guinness is brewed locally (local brewing being itself an example of a distributive option).

Clearly a number of channels are involved here. The product is sold in bottles and cans for home consumption as well as being sold in a variety of hospitality venues from bars to hotels. How to increase sales? Well one way is to increase the number of outlets in a particular channel, and one that makes best sense to promote – the Irish theme bar.

Guinness decided not only that the more Irish bars there are in far flung places the more Guinness they are likely to sell, but that the quality of those bars matters too – because that also influences sales. So Guinness exports ''Irishness'' by advising entrepreneurs on how to open an Irish pub and make it successful. A fully staffed dedicated department exists to do just this. They do not invest financially but advise, seeing the key issues as ensuring:

» *authentic look and atmosphere;*
» *authentic artifacts* (all those bits and bobs in a bar I visited in Kuala Lumpur recently probably came from the Guinness warehouse);
» *the right Irish food and music; and*
» *at least a core of trained staff from Ireland.*

They offer practical help and assistance in all these areas. It is a worthwhile activity. For example, there are nearly 50 Irish pubs in Germany (a country renowned for its own beer) and more than half the beer sold in such establishments is Irish. This example not only illustrates control of a channel of distribution, but also of helping to create it. Cheers.

Lastly the product must match local conditions. We see Guinness advertised as being good served and drunk cool these days, and the product has been changed to make it so, but how much of this is just for the great British summer? One suspects that also of importance is the number of countries in which Guinness is sold and promoted where the climate is markedly warmer than in the UK.

SUMMARY

It is clear that any extended scale imposed by international operations:

» makes for a more complex situation and thus a greater need to select a manageable mix of distributive methods and channels; and
» demands more, and more elaborate, communications around the network to ensure everything works smoothly.

Careful utilization of distributive methods and channels makes possible a scale of operation that prevents an otherwise major element of potential business going untapped.

The State of the Art

"Channels exist to serve consumers. Their purpose is similar to that of brands. Both exist to build superior customer value very efficiently for above average profits."

Hugh Davidson, author "Even more Offensive Marketing"

The following is probably in essence a common occurrence. I am considering adding a scanner to the computer equipment in my small office. My main requirement is that it will scan text *and* allow it to be converted into a Word document and be edited. I visit several specialist outlets. All have a range of machines on show. Will they do this? No one knows! There is no offer to find out or to try it and see (if they could demonstrate it, I would buy one on the spot). I retreat back to the office and telephone a large computer firm, the manufacturer of some of the machines that I have been looking at. Told of what occurred they express no surprise whatsoever. They do offer a demonstration in their own premises, but I am still trying to find the time to attend (actually I am trying to think of an easier way of proceeding!).

This does not seem to me to be an example of a distributive channel working well, and perhaps of one being badly managed too. So just what exactly should occur here?

Marketing is a core business function. It links the organization and the outside world in a variety of ways and acts as the catalyst to "bring in the business." An essential part of this is to create and maintain effective channels of distribution. The options here are wide and the part of the overall marketing activity necessary to ensure the right set up is significant. However, if the complexity can be dealt with, and this side of marketing can be made to work well, then it can be a significant part of what creates success in the market place.

THE NEED FOR DISTRIBUTION

However much any product or service delivers good value, however well it is promoted and however much customers – and potential customers – want it, it has to be in a position which gives them easy access to it; it must be distributed. And this can be a complex business, though it is certainly a marketing variable, albeit one that some businesses regard as rather more fixed than, in fact, it is.

Consider the variety of ways in which goods are made available. Consumer products are sold in shops – retailers, but these may vary enormously in nature, from supermarkets and department stores, to specialist retailers, general stores and more – even market traders. These may, in turn, be variously located: in a town or city center, in an out of town shopping area, in a multi-story shopping center, or on a neighborhood corner site. Even the simplest product can be sold through a bewildering range of outlets; see box.

THE AVAILABILITY OPTIONS

Products may be available very widely. Consider a simple everyday example of a chocolate bar like a *Kit Kat*. Outlets where this may be bought include the following:

» grocery and provision stores of all sorts and all types of super-market; and
» large and small, confectioners, newsagents, petrol stations, cinemas and other entertainment centers (e.g. bowling rink), leisure centers and clubs, some pubs and bars, vending machines, cafés, sandwich shops, and more.

To this one could add a list of different locations for some of these that would include the high street, railway and bus stations, out of town shopping centers and – again – more. This is very different from an example like *Wedgewood china*, which is sold through exclusive dealers and might be available in only one shop in a particular town.

But the complexity does not stop there, retailers may be supplied by a network of wholesalers or distributors, or they may simply not be involved; some consumer products are sold by mail order, or door to door, or through home parties (like Tupperware).

A similar situation applies to services, even traditional banking services being made available in stores, from machines in the street and through post and telephone – even on a drivein basis. Banking is also an example of the changes going on in the area of distribution, many of these developments being comparatively recent moves away from solely traditional branch operations. Business to business, industrial products are similarly complex in the range of distributive options they use.

Areas where change has occurred, or is occurring, can prompt rapid customer reaction if whatever new means are offered are found to be convenient. Old habits may die hard, but if change is made attractive and visible then new practices can be established and then these too can quickly become the norm. An instance is the rapid uptake of Internet shopping in some sectors; see Chapter 4 for more detail.

Conversely, if a distribution method is inconvenient for customers then they will seek other ways of access to the product (or simply not buy it), though sometimes inconveniences are tolerated because need is high, or is compensated for by other factors. For example, there are some who will put up with queues in one shop only because the alternative is too far away, or has nowhere convenient to park nearby.

How a company analyses the distributive possibilities and organizes to utilize a chosen method or methods effectively is certainly important to overall marketing success. But first it is important to consider how others – the various kinds of organization acting as distributors – operate and what they offer as a marketing resource.

THE CASE FOR DISTRIBUTORS

There are, in fact, a number of good reasons for delegating what is an essential element of the marketing mix.

» Distributive intermediaries provide a readymade network of contacts that would otherwise take years to establish at what might be a prohibitive cost; clearly even a large company might balk at the thought of setting up their own chain of specialist shops, and the incidence of this is very low.

» Distributors are objective and are not tied to one product. They can offer a range that appeals to their customers, electing to pitch this wide or narrow (and there some shops which sell very narrow ranges, e.g. only – ties, books on sport, coffee etc. and literally nothing else).

» Distributors provide an environment that the customer needs in order to make a choice. If different competing brands need to be compared, then this can be conveniently done by the customer in an outlet offering a range of similar products. If a distributor stocks a product and is also well known as an organization, with an attractive image, this may enhance the overall attractiveness of the shopping experience in the eyes of a consumer by association. In many fields allowing potential customers to view a wide choice – as in, say, selecting a television set – is, in fact, an important aspect of encouraging sales.

» Distributors can spread the costs of stocking and selling one product over all the items they carry, thereby distributing it at a lower cost than a supplier operating alone.

» The cost of bad debts is sometimes lower than it would be otherwise, as the distributor effectively shares the risk (however it may seem sometimes! - slow payment seems endemic in so many industries).

» Since the distributor is rewarded by a discount off the selling price, no capital is tied up by the principal in holding local stocks, though overlong credit can (does?) dilute this effect.

» Distributors can have good specialist knowledge of retailing or distribution, which the principal may not possess; or they should have – this clearly varies across different kinds of retailer.

So far so good, but there is another side to the coin. There can be conflicts of interest between principals and distributors.

DISTRIBUTIVE DOWNSIDES

There are a number of potential problems presented by distributors.

» They are not as committed to a particular product as its producer is. If the customer prefers another, they will substitute it. For example if a customer asks for advice in a travel agency, saying – "I want to arrange a weekend break and I see there are some good deals in France" - they are just as likely to end up finding themselves going to the Channel Isles. As the conversation progressed, the agent had no particular axe to grind in selling one destination rather than another – and in some cases discount structures may lead them to make particular recommendations that benefit them. In this case perhaps the company whose advertising successfully brought the customer into the shop in the first place, loses out.

» They may use the manufacturer's product for their own promotional purposes, something that is often linked to price cutting; not every product whose price is cut wants it (a manufacturer may feel it dilutes image, but be powerless to stop it being done, though see Chapter 3 for news of legal battles).

» They may drop the product from their list if they believe they can make a better profit with another line, this will clearly affect directly competing lines.

» Many distributors expect the manufacturer to stimulate demand for the product; for example, by advertising or providing display material. Sometimes they are more interested in the support than the product itself.

» Many distributors are tough on both terms (draconian is a word one hears regularly from some suppliers!) and have complex, time consuming, ordering procedures. At the same time they distance themselves from collaboration that could perhaps increase sales for both parties (with chains, significant decisions are "made at HQ" and sales representatives are left dealing in individual stores with young, inexperienced staff who do not know whether it is Tuesday or breakfast – perhaps I exaggerate, I hasten to add; well, a little).

The question of whether to deal direct with the consumer is, therefore, dependent first upon the availability of suitable channels and the willingness of buyers within them to add additional products to the range they sell; secondly, on balancing the economies of the distributors' lower selling and servicing costs with the disadvantages of not being present at the point where customers are making their decisions, and thus having less control over the selling process. Realistically, many companies have no option but to go through existing channels (whether these involve shops or not), though exactly how this is done and the mix involved can be varied. In addition, more radical variants may need to be found and run alongside (and without alienating) the retail chain; this can certainly be a way of increasing business.

WHAT CHANNEL OF DISTRIBUTION TO CHOOSE

There is no one easy and obvious route for most suppliers. A mix of methods needs setting up, and any decision must be based on facts and analysis. Although this is, as we have seen already, a decision involving some complex, interlocking issues, six main factors will influence the route taken:

1. Customer characteristics

Distributors are generally required when customers are widely dispersed; there are a large number of them and they buy frequently in small amounts. This is certainly true of many sectors of every day product, less so or not at all with regard to more specialist items.

2. Product characteristics

Direct distribution is required when bulky or heavy products are involved. Bulky products need channel arrangements that minimize the shipping distance and the number of times they need to be handled; even a brief look at physical distribution costs shows the importance of this factor.

Where high unit value can cover higher unit selling costs, then any manufacturer can keep control over distribution by dealing direct; as with certain off the page or catalogue distribution systems, or at the far end of the spectrum the likes of those who sell door to door. Finally, products requiring installation or maintenance are generally sold through a limited network, such as sole agents.

3. Distributor characteristics

Distributors are more useful when their skills of low cost contact, service and storage are more important than their lack of commitment to one product or brand. If very specific support is necessary then other options may be preferred.

4. Competitive characteristics

The channels chosen may often be influenced by the channels competitors use, and there may be dangers in moving away too far and too fast from what a market expects and likes. The competitive interaction in this way between retailers is another variable. In the area of fast food, Burger King try to obtain sites near to McDonalds, on the other hand, some manufacturers, such as Avon Cosmetics, choose not to compete for scarce positions in retail stores and have established profitable door-to-door direct selling operations instead. Similarly, major chains may seek to open branches near existing smaller, independent, retailers, not only to take advantage of their market knowledge – they are in an area where there is a demand – but with the aim of replacing them altogether. This last may well not be entirely in customers' interests and illustrates one aspect of the sheer power of major retailing groups.

5. Company characteristics

The size of a company often correlates with its market share. The bigger its market share, the easier it is to find distributors willing to handle the product – thus even a small shop is likely to find a corner for major brands, and will be more selective about what else they stock. They may not be able to stock everything, but will find space for anything they believe in. Where there is clearly profit to be made no-one wants to miss out on it. Similarly, a supplier may be innovative (and/or build on a strength) and seek ways of becoming less dependent on the normal chain of distribution.

Creativity may have a role to play here. For instance, cosmetics may sell well in outlets that simply display them, but stores putting on make-up demonstrations (or letting the manufacturer do so) may create an edge, for a while.

Additionally, a policy of fast delivery is less compatible with a large number of stages in the channel and there is a danger that slow delivery (measured in market terms) dilutes marketing effectiveness. As service standards increase so there is less room for anyone that lags behind to do as well as they might – slow delivery is increasingly not acceptable. This has been a problem for some in e-tailing. The instant nature of the purchasing process seems to prompt feelings in consumers that delivery should be swift – a feeling encouraged by those who do just that. Distance (and, for some people, the still new method) can reduce credibility and trust; one bad experience of delay is enough to rule out any repeat business (especially if checking up on any pending matters is difficult too).

6. Environmental characteristics

Changes in the economic and legal environment can also bring about changes in distributive structures. For example, when the market is depressed, manufacturers want to move their goods to market in the most economic way. They thus cut out intermediaries or unessential services to compete on price and deal direct. Again, legal restrictions have been introduced in the UK in recent years to prevent any channel characteristics which may weaken competition.

Also influencing how things are done are overall trends within retailing. Out of town shopping, the use of the car (or restrictions on it), and everything from the cost of renting retail accommodation to the desirability of an area, all influence the likelihood of shoppers patronizing a particular area, and thus a particular shop. Certainly this may influence where all sorts of product are bought, and this in turn may influence what is bought.

An example might be the development of Covent Garden vegetable market in London. Now an attractive area of restaurants and entertainment as well as shops it attracts people from far and wide. Someone might well buy something, a present perhaps, in a shop there, choosing something different from what they might have bought if they had shopped somewhere else. Such decisions are based on what is there, how it is displayed and more.

A major retailing trend is towards out of town shopping centers of various sorts. In some, small independent shops fit in well. In others – blocks of the big retail groups (Sainsburys, Dixons, etc.) predominate and the environment is not right for the small shopkeeper.

The bigger the environmental change the more likely it is to have repercussions, and there are doubtless plenty of changes still to come in this area.

VARIETY AND CHANGE

Usually it is possible to identify several different types of channel or distributors. In certain industries some of the alternatives may be further from standard practice than others, but that does not mean they are not worthy of consideration, or cannot be part of the distribution mix. Things that are normal now may have originally been difficult to establish. For example, many in business know and deal with Wyvern Books who sell business titles, like this one, by direct mail, sending tiny cards in packs of 20-30 in one envelope. This had not been done in such a way before, and was viewed with some skepticism by some involved at the outset; not only does it work well, but the number of cards included in one "shot" has grown since its inception, and sales with it.

Some companies are, of course, bound to the standard form in their field, but the point here is that it pays to remain open minded; channels may change little, traditional routes may remain the most important, creating the greatest volume of business, but other possibilities may still create some growth.

There are still without doubt many new possible innovations in prospect for distribution (the Internet to name but one of current interest) and things that seem unlikely today will no doubt be looked back on in years to come as entirely normal. We all have 20/20 hindsight. The trick for suppliers is to make sure some marketing time, effort and thinking goes into exploring and testing new methods. This is, of course, true of most things, but distribution is a prime candidate for the very reason that many do see it as essentially static, at least in the short term. Perhaps this just means there is all the more possibility of using it to steal an edge over more conservative competitors.

So, alternatives need be explored to see which channel or combination of channels best meets the firm's objectives and constraints. However, the best choice of channel must take into account the degree to which the company can control, or at least influence, the distribution channel created. But first, it is important that any channel works from the point of view of *customers*.

SERVICE TO CUSTOMERS

Brands exist to create superior customer value and thus maximize profit opportunities. Channels have a similar role; they should provide not just a route along which products and services are made available, but should actively create availability in a way that provides customers with a satisfactory – indeed, for consumer goods, interesting, perhaps even exciting – way of obtaining what they want.

As such, channels must be judged on the basis of how well they deliver their "package" of service benefits. To define this think about what a channel provides under the following headings:

» *convenience*: such factors as how much time is taken up (so things like being nearby, easy parking and having sensible opening hours) etc;

» *range*: choice and mix of what is available, allied products etc;

» *price*: value in price terms, includes all aspects of price (e.g. discounts, payment terms);

» *quality*: overall value including price and service;

» *service*: customer care attitudes and practice, and advice if necessary (includes indirect service factors such as the provision of lavatories in a shopping mall);

» *environment*: everything from style to cleanliness, also ease of use (e.g. pushchair friendly?) and level of crowds;

» *identification*: clarity of purpose (e.g. is a shopping center all high price or the reverse – for instance, saying "factory outlets" clearly identifies what is in store at least in a general sense); and

» *image*: in the overall sense of *projecting* such factors as quality, the kind of person to whom it is directed etc.

Note that channels are subject to the segmentation just as much as products. A channel may well focus on a part, sometimes a tightly focused part, of a total market. Thus in terms of both price and people channels may be designed to attract in different ways. Thus you can, for example, buy your new kitchen packed flat in boxes from a chain store at an out of town shopping center, or have someone come to your home and advise and supply you individually, before installing it for you.

Additionally, the channel can be used directly to enhance image, for example:

» up market theme pubs featuring more expensive "designer" beers and specialty drinks use the quality or trendy image to tie in with the appeal of individual products;

» the restricted availability of a top brand of perfume or fine china, sold only through a small number of exclusive dealerships, enhances their image of desirability; and

» even a humble loaf sold in a small "real" bakery has sufficient added appeal to command a premium price.

At the end of the day what works for consumers is the ultimate measure. A channel will not continue to operate successfully without the approval of the customers who patronize it (unless they have no alternative, in which case it is vulnerable to competitive forces).

POWERFUL DISTRIBUTIVE FORCES

When few companies dominate an area of distribution, then they can wield considerable power. In The US and in the UK, amongst other markets, this is certainly dramatically the case in food marketing. If you sell a branded food product in the UK then most of your retail market will go through just five organizations whose chains of shops make up some 80% of the market. Miss out on one and a very significant amount of the potential market is lost.

This gives such organizations considerable power (see box), and delicate negotiations may be necessary to create a balance that gives a sound basis for doing business to both parties. In such a situation margins are constantly under pressure and yet there is a need to support the buyers in a way that enhances the business opportunities inherent in the chain concerned.

DISTRIBUTOR POWER
The kinds of thing a manufacturer might be pressed on include:

» additional time from the field sales force (for instance to help merchandising);
» discounts (and there may be many different bases for them, e.g. quantity bought or when purchase is made; and some are retrospective);
» any special packaging and packing;
» delivery (maybe to multiple locations, labeling; credit terms (and beyond);
» returns and damage arrangements;
» advertising and promotional support;
» merchandising materials;
» training of customers' staff; and
» financing (including special credit terms).

These sorts of cost are, of course, all in addition to normal production and distribution costs. Yet major players can make demands here that quickly put margins under pressure, knowing that the pressure for the supplier to maintain a relationship with them is intense. On the other side, a buyer – say a retailer – does not want to alienate a supplier and miss the opportunity of profiting from selling a good product. So realistically a balance is necessary; it is however one that the supplier may sometimes think is tending to be one sided.

In some fields, for example foods, many suppliers may feel that they are too much at the beck and call of the retailers, especially the large ones. Large customers need careful handling; they are not just different in size, they are different in nature. This links to the area of key account management, which is outside the remit of this work (but which is touched on in the Express-Exec on *Sales Management*).

Thus the first stage of channel management is to select the right channel or, more likely, to select and balance the right mix of channels. The second is to make your use of it as effective as possible.

IT'S A DEAL

Many arrangements with distributors are contractual. This is not a legal nicety, it is imperative to have the detail right and, in international operations, have it on a basis that is right, market by market. This is a technical area where the cost of specialist advice is well worthwhile.

In one European industrial component company, trading across the world through a long list of national distributors operating in their specialist industrial field, a review of the contractual arrangement across the operation was conducted. Arrangements had grown up over time. Markets had been gradually added and in each case a deal had been struck, by a range of different people at different times, to secure the services of what was regarded as the best local dealer with which to work.

As a result, not counting minor differences, 18 different forms of contract were found to be in force. Early ones in some cases still contained clauses and terms that were not easily compatible with current operations. Worse, distributors were themselves raising issues – particularly of the unfairness of their arrangement compared with another – and this was leading to time-consuming and costly renegotiating. The whole thing needed to be sorted into some sort of order. Better to set a consistent policy in the first place, and have a regular review process in place from the beginning.

MANAGING CHANNELS

Not only are chosen distributors likely to work better on behalf of any manufacturer if communications, support (e.g. information, training, service and support) and motivation are good, but they will have their own ideas, and a good working relationship must be adopted if both are to profit from the partnership. At best, all this takes time, and often it is easy to simply see people as sources of revenue, rather than someone to work with. Yet the best may only be got from a market when the two parties do work, and work effectively, together.

Distribution is a key element in marketing, one that sometimes goes by default because existing methods are regarded as fixed, but where making existing arrangement work well – and seeking new or additional ones – can create further sale success.

Distribution is a vital process, and its channels link the company to customers, and thus marketing activity can be made or broken by its performance.

The right methods must be chosen, and then everyone down the line needs to be worked with effectively. Amongst retailers, few will even consider taking on a new product (or taking on board any idea) unless they can be convinced that the demand exists, and that its doing so is more that an optimistic gleam in a supplier's eye. They need to know which market segment the product is aimed at and whether it fits with their customer franchise. And exactly the same is true of industrial and other markets.

Working through any channel of distribution demands:

» clear policy; that all parties have clear, understood and agreed expectations of each other;
» clear terms of trade (discounts and all financial arrangements); and

» sufficient time and resources to be put into the ongoing process of managing, communicating with and motivating those organizations and people upon whom sales are ultimately dependent.

This latter area of communications, motivation and support is most important. It is not something that can be approached ad hoc. It needs a systematic and ongoing approach, one well tailored to the people on the receiving end of the communication (more about this appears in Chapter 5, where widespread global networks give it an especial priority).

SUMMARY

Selecting and managing channels of distribution demands analysis, decision and activity at every level;

» analyzing the market as a whole, how it operates and how it can, and might, be accessed;
» analyzing individual distribution channels to see how they fit with your activity and your marketing strategy;
» similarly analyzing how well they meet customer needs;
» selecting the right mix;
» prioritizing them in terms of the flow of business through each and the respective weight of activity that you will put behind each one;
» making suitable arrangements (and, if necessary, contracts) with the parties involved (wholesalers, distributors – whatever);
» creating and maintaining a relationship with them through a suitable communications program;
» planning and implementing individual key account strategies with all those individual customers who warrant attention at this level;
» reviewing performance and fine tuning activity as necessary; and
» thinking and acting creatively to find and explore new channels and new ways of making existing channels work more effectively in future.

There is always a range of channel options. Some are seen as "the norm," others as peripheral or "unlikely to work," still more we can as yet not anticipate. But whatever is done, whatever range of ways may be used together, this is an area that marketing must aim to influence. It is at the interface, whatever form that takes, that sales are ultimately made. So the supplier must work effectively with what is necessarily given (and this includes dealing with aspects of the business that you would rather were different), and also seek new approaches and methods where appropriate and take an innovative and creative approach to the whole process of distribution.

In Practice

"I think ideas are easy. It's execution that's hard. If you and I were to sit here for an hour and scribble on this chalk board on the wall, we could come up with a hundred good ideas. The hard part is making them work, and there are several key components in that."

Jeff Bezos, founder and CEO of Amazon.com

Channel management, like so much else in marketing, needs an active approach. Distribution is a multi-faceted and dynamic area, and what needs to be done relates to a number of levels. Dividing it into four parts categorizes it well.

» *Channel choice*: this is clearly the first stage. It is necessary to look at the channels available and how well they can serve the organization and its customers. It is useful to see whether the choice ought to include any new channels, or variants of traditional methods. It is sensible to review the options widely and not to be seduced into a quick decision about what is most obvious. It may be best to utilize a variety of channels, though some may be more important than others.

» *Working the channel mix*: on a regular basis the relative performance of the various channels used needs to be reviewed (see Chapter 8, about market maps). This allows changes to be initiated, for example so that one channel is given a new, and greater, priority or another is dropped or reduced in emphasis.

» *Enhancing channel performance*: the people and organizations that make up chosen channels need active, ongoing support and communication (this is reviewed in more detail in Chapter 6). The nature of this varies, of course. Marketing through distributors, especially internationally, needs careful individual communication across a wide spectrum from motivation to providing training support.

» *Auditing the overall process*: then, occasionally but regularly, an audit should be conducted on the total process. There are various ways of approaching such an exercise, but it can be encapsulated under the following headings:

  » *Channels*: taking a broad view of the channel system, mapping the flow through all the relevant channels, looking at the share of the market served by each and at the trends for the future;

» *Channel services*: looking at key service elements and how service compares with competitors; such a review would include taking a view of sales and technical support, customer service (and after sales service), and more;

» *Channel shares*: comparing the strategy and the proportion of business going through each channel, and looking at it alongside competitors;

» *Marketing resources*: comparing resources, such as manpower, distributors, sales offices etc. on a geographic basis and incorporating competitor comparisons; and

» *Concentration*: this means looking at all the ratios such as customer numbers and things like the implications of the 80/20 rule.

In this chapter we review a number of examples that span this whole process or have application within it. The first two sections describe cases showing the value of overall review and getting channel choice right.

JAPANESE MACHINERY (SANWA)

This case shows how complex arrangements can hide potential and how reviewing what needs to be done and tailoring a solution to it can maximize sales potential. Sanwa is a Japanese producer of machinery that is sold to different kinds of manufacturers. It sells directly to customers in Japan. For overseas markets, it had engaged a big Japanese trading company, Itochu, to handle the sales and service. During the past fifteen years, Sanwa had started to take over the functions of Itochu. The priority of which country or region to take on depends on the market potential, the market share Sanwa currently has and whether Sanwa can make a significant impact. Five years ago, Sanwa set up a representative office in Singapore to take over the regional territory from Itochu.

The Singapore office is responsible for ASEAN markets, and is headed by a local regional manager. On the surface, the sales in ASEAN markets look quite good. The regional manager started to analyze the market in more detail in the various markets. In particular, he looked into Indonesia. Itochu had appointed a sole distributor in Jakarta and the sales appear quite satisfactory. However, the market survey conducted by the regional manager found that the market potential is much bigger than they had expected. The current distributor in fact only covered a small part of the market. The distributor appointed dealers in several locations. Some of the dealers in turn appointed agents to handle the sales.

Functions of successful distributors

To be successful in marketing Sanwa machines, analysis showed that any distributor needs to perform the following functions:

» offer customers complete solutions using Sanwa as the core machine;
» have the capability to do system integration;
» have a strong in-house support team to provide expertise in technical matters, application, installation and service;
» have the capability to sell on quality and performance, not price; and
» be able to provide demonstration and test samples.

It was found that the sole distributor was weak in most of the above areas and, though sub-agents met these criteria to some degree, the full sales potential was clearly not being realized.

Results

Because of the vast territory and many fragmented market segments, the regional manager sacked the distributor and appointed a country representative to oversee the whole Indonesian market. The country representative was given the mandate to appoint different distributors to cover the vast territory and the many market segments. Each distributor was selected based on their strength in the market segments where they had the competence and connection. As a result of this decision, Sanwa was able to achieve the same sales result of the previous distributor within the first year of this change and thereafter went on to continuous growth for many years.

The second case is also set in Asia.

CONTINENTAL AIR CONDITIONING EQUIPMENT

This company has been selling very well through an exclusive distributor in Thailand and enjoying steady growth for the past several years.

Its customers are office and commercial buildings, factories, department stores, retail shops and upper class residences. For small jobs, the distributor has a dealer network that covers the whole market geographically and does so very well. The dealers buy Continental equipment from the distributor and then sees to installation in their customers' premises. For bigger jobs, the dealers do not have the resources to handle them. In order to address this market segment, the distributor sets up a wholly-owned contracting company to buy and install the Continental equipment.

The Problem

The above situation has worked well for Continental and the distributor for the past few years. However, the market is never static and changes have been happening.

1 As the dealers grow, they become bigger and start to compete against the wholly-owned contracting arm of the distributor. The dealers feel that they are at a disadvantage as the distributor is likely to favor its wholly-owned contractor with favorable pricing for the equipment.
2 As the market becomes bigger, the mechanical and electrical designs for bigger buildings are increasingly being handled by professional engineers. Mechanical consultants are starting to emerge and be engaged by the building owners. They design the air conditioning system of the building and specify the types of air conditioning equipment to be installed in the building.
3 At the same time, independent air conditioning contractors are starting to emerge in the market place. These are air conditioning contractors specializing in bidding and installing for the big buildings and are not tied to any specific brands of air conditioning equipment. They will be competing with the wholly-owned contracting arm of the distributor as well as the bigger dealers who are starting to bid on the bigger jobs.

Results

To remain a dominant player in the air conditioning market in Thailand and maintain its market share, Continental decided to take an active role in Thailand. It first took a controlling interest in the Thai distributor.

It saw its future in developing the dealer network. In order to do that, it had to divest and close the wholly-owned contracting subsidiary. To address the growing influence of the mechanical consultants, it sets up a specialist team of highly qualified engineers to influence the technical specifications of their projects. This will minimize the price war initiated by the independent air conditioning contractors who do not have any brand loyalty. There is the bonus of a lucrative income from servicing contracts of an increasing base of installations.

This change of channel strategy with a series of successive tactics enabled Continental to preserve its predominant position in the market.

DISPLAY AND MERCHANDISING

Now, an example of another area of general application, especially within retail channels. The application of display is wide ranging. It has relevance in industrial and business-to-business marketing, for example in showrooms. But here we will investigate it in its main context linked to retailing, where it provides an example of one aspect of channel management designed specifically for improving the flow of business.

A store display has clear objectives. Research confirms they are a key influence on purchasing decisions. They are designed to do specific things.

» *Sell more*: That is to sell a quantity over and above the level that would occur if no action were taken. Some people will always want certain products and will search them out.
» *Inform*: For example, telling customers that a shop is there, indicating something of the range of products it sells, highlighting what is new, directing people to the right section etc.
» *Persuade*: Making the message attractive, understandable and convincing – to prompt sales.

Display has to convey messages to many different groups of people, particularly:

» those who may pass the shop by, who will not even enter unless something external catches their eye;
» those who come into the shop for one small item and who may buy more, and the ubiquitous "browser." This is one reason most shops

sell a mixture of things, to maximize the number of people they attract; and

» those who are active or regular customers.

Thus, for example, a customer seeing a display of books labeled "for holiday reading" has their eye caught by perhaps one aspect of the display - a bucket and spade, say. They then move from thinking - "What's this?" to - "Perhaps I do need a book for my holiday" to - "That looks just the thing" to - "I'll buy it."

This is the essential principle behind good display, and checking a particular display to see if it will carry customers through this kind of sequence is a useful test of its likely effectiveness. So too is ringing the changes and surprising or intriguing people.

STORE LAYOUT

While many aspects are fixed, for a variety of reasons - cost, the lease will not allow change and so on - others are not. It is then a matter of detail. There are a number of factors, all of which can be organized in a way that influences sales. The detail, and the creativeness with which things are done, and creating a mix that works at any particular moment is what is important here. The boxed paragraph gives more detail of factors relating just to store layout.

BOOSTING BUSINESS IN-STORE

The following layout factors, listed in no particular order of importance, can all contribute.

Traffic flow
90 per cent of the population are righthanded and will turn accordingly on entering a shop and tend to go round it clockwise. (This is compounded by habit as so many supermarkets and department stores, recognizing this, encourage it - it has then become the norm with many of us.)

Eyes
Customers select most readily from goods displayed at eye level (generally 60-62 inches for a woman, a little higher for men). This

puts very high or low shelves at a corresponding disadvantage; and many shops have plenty of both in order to maximize utilization of space. There are problems here with the volume of stock to be carried and displayed, but customers may resent having to shop on their hands and knees. Manufacturers must spend part of their promotion and sales effort on securing space for their products in the prime locations.

Quantity

Customers buy more readily from things displayed in quantity, rather than a single example of a product, hence the piles of goods that are characteristic of many retailers, particularly supermarkets.

Vertical display

Products displayed together are found more manageable if they are above and below each other rather than arranged side by side.

Accident

Customers are less likely to pick up, or browse, from any layout that appears accident-prone. In other words, if they think they may not be able to balance an item back in position or that other items may fall, especially if they fear damaging something; especially if the something is fragile, valuable or both. And this is important because in certain shops the customer needs to pick up and inspect the product; indeed they may not be prepared to buy without doing so.

Choice

Customers are attuned to choice. A number of options make this easy to exercise, products sell better from within a range of similar items.

Relationships

Customers expect to find related items close at hand (for example, pens, pencils and paper go naturally together; something like strawberries and cream might seem to go in different areas – fruit and dairy products – but will sell well together).

Cash points/service points/cash tills

These need to be convenient and clearly indicated (and, of course, promptly and helpfully manned; but that is another issue) and can be a focal point for some display.

Position

In a large shop, people will walk or search further for things they feel are essential (thus it is no accident that bread and sugar are normally at the rear of the supermarket). So, if the children's toys are up three flights of stairs, mothers with buggies/pushchairs/prams will not make that shop first choice.

Color

Color has a fashion, and an image, connotation – bright may be seen as brash – so it must be carefully chosen. This applies to display materials, for example a backcloth in the window as well as decoration. Too dull, however, and things are not noticed.

Lighting

The lighting must be good – perhaps especially in shops where clear vision of, say, color of a product is important – if something cannot be found or seen clearly no one will buy it, and people's patience is limited.

Seating

Some stores want to encourage browsing so, if lack of space does not prohibit, they provide some chairs and perhaps a stool near the till for older customers.

Background *music*

This can evoke strong opinions. Some like it, some hate it. However, the reverse, a librarylike silence, can be off putting for some. Certainly careful choice and consideration of volume level is necessary. Some seem to favor relaxing, predominantly classical and soft jazz, music that may become very much part of their overall style. Others go for a brasher approach.

Character

Part of the overall atmosphere will come from the main physical elements of the shop, dark wooden paneling has a quite different feel to more modern alternatives (both may have their place).

Flooring

This will be noticed. Is it quiet? Can it be kept clean easily? And does it (or should it) direct customer flow as some shops do, using different colors for pathways?

Reach

If things are out of reach, people are reluctant to "be a nuisance" by asking and may not buy.

Signage

Again, as people are reluctant to ask, there must be sufficient signs and all must be clear and direct people easily to everything in the shop. In addition, many signs are virtually instore advertisements and these can be used to good effect. This is an area first for clarity, but that can also be creatively used in a shop. This is another area where simple ideas and variety can be useful. With control of image in mind some retailers go their own way and have their own signs and posters in their stores. Others take and use material from their suppliers (another aspect of marketing is to make what is offered attractive and desirable).

Standing space

Space to stand and look without completely blocking "traffic" flow may encourage purchase. This links to cost; lower rental, out of town shops may well have more space to play with.

Security

Last, but by no means least, this is sadly important in every aspect of retailing. Visibility in terms of, for example, closed circuit TV (CCTV) that may be used, is important. So too is simple vigilance. Retailing is unfortunately rarely sufficiently profitable to sustain a high level of pilferage without concern.

This list is not, of course, comprehensive (and related factors such as window displays can be added), but these and other factors are all important with the overall physical construction and layout acting as the backcloth to any display, in the shop or in the window.

Looking at this sort of area in a little detail shows clearly the breadth of activities that channel management encompasses. Whatever the channel, and whatever the entity involved – from retailers to specialist overseas agents – activity can be organized that enhances the effectiveness. Display and merchandising are a case in point. In the retail area reviewed, unless retailers are owned, then the prime mover in this area is the retailer. Some brook no "interference," they organize things; in the UK Dixons is an example of this – all the promotional material used in-store is their own and they will accommodate none from their suppliers. More welcome assistance, and providing this and providing it better than competitors, is a way of creating an edge – making a particular channel work better for one supplier than another.

OLD AND NEW

As another example of channel management in action, and to show how old and new elements of distribution can work together, I would mention Hyphone. But let us first consider a problem. Many people visit the web sites of the new e-tailers and companies dealing direct, they are interested, they take time to log on and browse the site – but they do not buy. Why not?

There may be numbers of very different reasons. They do not cope in some way with the technology, something interrupts them, or sitting alone they lack the confidence to take the final step. They are not convinced it is the deal for them or they have some point of enquiry unresolved. It is the point at which, in a retailer, a sales assistant offering immediate identification of the problem, questions and advice to deal with it might well prompt the deal to be struck.

Technology company Byzantium think Hyphone is the answer. The system allows a button (or many buttons) to be included as an integral part of a web site. A potential customer clicking on the button, activates a process that puts them in touch with a call center and are able to talk to someone over the PC (on the same line connecting them to the site). They can ask questions, and the company representative can provide answers; and, of course, the site can be used as a visual aid. The customer can be guided to specific pages and ultimately guided to click the button that completes a purchase. Additional features allow forms to be filled by the customer simply dictating notes to be made on a whiteboard device as the conversation proceeds; and others will no doubt be added.

New as I write, Hyphone is already being taken up by major companies (Chase de Vere, Barclays and US optician 20rx, for instance), you will probably come across it soon. It is more than a conversion device, it combines technology and good, old fashioned personal service in a way that customers seem to like. In effect it is creating another new channel that combines elements of old ones and recent ones to produce something more powerful. Perhaps this is the future. Certainly it reinforces the overall principle that whatever channel management does, it must do it in a way that gives customers an experience they find efficient, convenient and pleasant.

DEALER UPGRADE

Now an example of how one organization acted to get the most from a distributor network in business to business marketing channels.

In the highly competitive office equipment market Sharp marketed its products through dealers, largely smaller independent operations who were weaker in accessing the corporate market buyers more used to dealing direct with suppliers like Xerox or Cannon. Setting high growth targets, Sharp, set about upgrading their dealers. The set up a quality measure – the Sharp Integrated Quality Standard (SIQS) – configured to incorporate general standards like ISO 9002, and to reflect what was necessary in areas of marketing, sales, human resources and health and safety, quality, service and customer satisfaction. This was something for which dealers had to qualify, a process that involved them in signing up to a 3-day audit of their business which was carried out by independent consultants. Although the process was subsidized, the dealers were expected to pay some of the cost. The vast majority took up the option and most qualified for SIQS status.

In this way the manufacturer addressed matters in two separate, yet interrelated, ways. They increased the business skills that the dealers could bring to bear on selling their product, and they improved the image of the dealers, making them entities with whom corporate customers found it acceptable to deal. Overall sales rose, with the proportion of business coming from corporate customers increasing in line with their goal.

The first decision here was to develop and upgrade the network (and reject other options like extending their own sales resource and selling direct). The second was to undertake an integrated initiative to create the change required – and to make it acceptable (one suspects dealer motivation benefited alongside the practical changes).

The cost and commitment necessary to set up, and successfully see through such a scheme, is manifest. Again it illustrates just how much there is to gain by taking the right approach to the whole question of channels and acting to maximize their effectiveness.

INITIATING CHANNEL CHANGE

For a final word let us turn to the example of a service, banking, and specifically to changes that took banking into something of a revolution in recent years. There have been many influences including the need to both reduce costs and increase profits. The result has been a world of banking that is leagues away from the old traditional picture, and what has changed most is the nature of the distribution channel used and how it is managed.

To recap: once upon a time everyone with a current account at a bank dealt through a branch. You visited it personally for routine transactions like drawing out or paying in cash, and politely asked for an appointment with the manager if you wanted a loan. Then a new bank, First Direct, was set up, as a division of Midland Bank (now HSBC, following the merger with Hong Kong Shanghai Banking Corporation), its operation based on changing all this. They set out to persuade people that they did not need branches – First Direct had none – but that dealing with your bank by telephone was the thing to do. Electronic machines – the ubiquitous "hole in the wall machine" – allowed cash to be withdrawn and most everything else could be done on the telephone. In sounds odd now, but I for one was wary at the time. Ring up, say "Pay this bill" and be confident it would be done? Never. Except that, after not very long, people said "Yes."

First Direct's customer numbers grew and they can rightly claim to have led the revolution that followed.

What happened is interesting. The bank moved forward on two fronts. First to reduce the costs of servicing accounts, largely by negating the need for branches, and secondly by creating a competitive edge by giving customers something they wanted. To begin with they might not have known what they wanted, but they did know something about the way they did *not* want bank services delivered. They did not want long periods of time wasted queuing in branches, or opening hours that suited only the bank, or to wait forever while their request for a loan went through several unexplained stages before any answer was forthcoming. Not to mention all the attendant problems of visiting a branch, the time, the parking and . . . enough.

They quickly found the new system worked well – for the most part First Direct have always delivered excellent service and made the telephone relationship seem very *personal*. The proliferation of call centers since has diluted overall standards and made the best seem even better. Effectively a new channel was created, along with product changes to make it fit. Its profile was fresh and modern and matched busy lifestyles; if you wanted to pay your bills in the middle of the night you now could. Service and the new channel were inextricably linked, and the bank linked also to sales (for example cross selling insurance alongside providing travelers checks and making the chatty approach sound like service, not sales).

It is an example of real innovation, of sensitivity to customer needs and the power of backing an idea with appropriate service. What is more it has not stood still, additional services were quickly added, for example share dealing. And you can now access your account as easily over the Internet as by telephone. Other banks, of course, followed suit and most offer this kind of service now, but First Direct remain synonymous with telephone banking and still conjures up a quality image in most peoples' minds. Excuse me I must phone and see if my royalty check has arrived.

A LOOK AHEAD

Despite what Niels Bohr said (*Prediction is always difficult, especially of the future*), it is nevertheless perhaps worth setting out a few examples of likely changes in a random selection of distributive situations. Bear in mind that, with the ability to buy almost anything without leaving home, it will have to be made more attractive to shop.

» Bookshops already have cafés, in future they will have more events to attract people in store (this concept applies to other retailers too).
» Newspapers, and perhaps magazines, will be delivered electronically (with the ability for a customer to omit, or only take, certain parts or information on certain topics).
» Supermarkets will deliver staple items (from tissues to dog food) and become more specialized, providing a place for those items that need real choice or tasting, like wine and cheese.
» Increasingly interactive Internet sites will extend the kind of product bought this way (a good virtual tour of a house or the banqueting suite being considered for a wedding would cut out a lot of shopping around).
» Service standards will have to increase in retail environments to continue to provide reason for customers to use them.

In addition, one change will create another. If renting a movie no longer involves going out to pick up a video tape or DVD disk (because it comes down a telephone line or cable), what about other purchases made on such visits? What will increased motoring costs, including city center motoring tolls, do to popular choices for shopping? If more people work at home will home sales visits, catalogue selling and other such methods increase?

Distribution is definitely an area that needs watching and to which most organizations will have to adapt, and some will succeed through innovation.

SUMMARY

There is nothing wrong with using traditional channels, but – as was hinted at above – even they are changing. In a dynamic world perhaps the key things are to:

» review all the options;
» choose wisely (based on fact and analysis) and create a mix that works for you;

» actively manage the people and organizations down the chain on whom you depend; and

» innovate: find and try new ways (and keep up with what other people are introducing or experimenting with).

Key Concepts and Thinkers

"Many businessmen – especially makers of industrial products –
are as unaware that they use distribution channels, let alone that
they depend on them, as Molière's Monsieur Jourdain was that he
spoke prose."

Peter Drucker, author and management guru

GLOSSARY

Channel level – Essentially this is the equivalent of a market segment
in channel terms, a portion of the channel that can be dealt with
through a common approach, or, as Philip Kotler has put it: "A layer
of intermediaries that performs some work in bringing the product
and its ownership closer to the final buyer."

Channel of distribution – The route taken by a product, or a service,
as it passes from producer to consumer (the term distributive chain
is also used).

Direct marketing – Method of distributing products directly to consumers, without the use of intermediaries such as wholesalers and
retailers; it can involve any kind of product or service.

Disintermediation – What a word! It just means a simplification of
the channels of distribution for a particular company or product, for
example involving concentrating on some routes to the exclusion of
others.

Distribution centre – A large in some industries highly automated
warehouse designed to receive goods (most usually products rather
than services) from various suppliers, take orders, fulfill them efficiently and deliver goods to customers as quickly as possible

Distribution network – The network is the particular combination of
channels used by any one producer. The words network, channels
and chains of distribution have similar meanings and choice of one
rather than another indicates no great descriptive difference.

Drop shippers – Agents of some sort who sell on behalf of a principle
but never take possession of the goods, which go direct from
producer to customer.

Dual branding – The specific tactic of producing two different products, using two different brand names and intended to be sold
through different channels. For example, Seiko watches have a sub-
brand Alba sold in outlets of lower quality than that for the main

brand, though there is some, presumably intentional, overlap with the top of one range appearing alongside the lower part of the other.

Dual distribution – The use of two major and contrasting channels to sell the same product, in the way that pens are sold through retailers and business to business for use as corporate gifts.

Exclusive distribution – Giving a small number of outlets of whatever sort the right to be "exclusive dealers" or stockists. The right usually carries responsibilities (for example to hold guaranteed minimum stocks) and links to marketing that makes a positive point about the system; a product example is fine china.

Exhibitions – These from trade shows to public exhibitions can be themselves a specialized channel and, for some organizations, are their only way of interfacing with customers. They can be large like an annual national event, or small like a local craft fair.

Franchising – A method of providing a distribution channel by arrangement with someone who is given the right to sell the product, usually under strict terms and conditions regarding how it done.

Functional middlemen – Intermediaries who do not take title of products resold (see Merchants, who do).

Gray products (and gray imports) – Products obtained unofficially through dubious byways of distribution to allow them to be offered for sale at a lower price than the manufacturer would wish and see as compatible with protecting brand image.

Horizontal marketing system – A channel arrangement that involves two or more companies on the same level of distribution joining or working together.

Intermediaries – Any firms which act as a link between producers and consumers in the channel of distribution (thus retailers, wholesalers, distributors etc. are all intermediaries; so too may be organizations that have only recommendatory influence).

Merchants – Intermediaries who take title to products before selling them on.

Middleman – Another term for intermediaries.

Multiple marketing channels – The use of several marketing channels simultaneously, usually used only when there is a radical difference, for example a chemical company using different channels to sell weed killer to farmers and to those with domestic gardens.

Manufacturers – Manufacturers or producers of products and services are the starting point for all channels of distribution; which exist to get their output to market.

Mass exclusivity – What appears like a contradiction in terms is, in fact, a neat expression describing careful positioning. A product enjoying mass exclusivity is thought to be more special, and less widely known and available than it actually is. If this can be achieved it gives some of the advantages of exclusive distribution *and* wider tactics.

Physical distribution – Included here to avoid confusion, physical distribution is the process of physically transporting goods from point of origin to point of sale. That may sound straightforward, but includes many associated factors from ensuring packaging that protects to the cost-effectiveness of different forms of transport and insurance, shipping and import taxes in export business.

Shelf life – Either the length of time a product (food products make a good example) remains fit for sale, or the average length of time it takes for a product to be sold, once it has been displayed for sale.

Shopping center – There are a whole range of different types of shopping center now operating, ranging from a group of shops under one roof in, or off the high street, to massive dedicated areas where major stores and others are grouped in out of town settings in a variety of combinations; many different terms seem to be used malls, retail parks etc. without very precise definition or difference.

Supply chain management – This phrase is a distinct variant on channel management, it describes *co-operative* working among some combination of producers, suppliers and distributors (e.g. retailers) in a way designed for their mutual benefit.

Telemarketing – The direct selling of products or services via telephone contact that can either be cold calling or regular servicing of existing customers.

Vending – Sales through automatic dispensing machines (as, for example, on railway station platforms or in pubs); it can link to other channels or act in its own specialist right.

Vertical marketing system - This is a channel structure in which producers, wholesalers and retailers (or others) act together one level owns the next, is linked to them contractually or simply has so much power that they must work together.

Warehouse clubs (or discount sheds) - Large volume, small range outlets selling at keenly competitive discount prices to tightly targeted customer groups who must pay an annual membership fee (Costco is an example).

Wholesaler - Intermediaries who buy, hold stock and sell on most usually to retailers, though the term is also used in industrial marketing.

Vertical Marketing System (VMS) - "A distribution channel structure in which producers, wholesalers and retailers act as a unified system. One channel member owns the others, has contracts with them, or has so much power that they all co-operate." (Kotler, 1999, page 900.)

ELECTRONIC OPTIONS

The terminology here, with its proliferation of words involving the prefix "e," changes day by day. Essentially the key things here are that there are now a variety of *e-commerce* options. A customer can go *online shopping* or *Internet shopping* at an *e-tailer* (that is the electronic equivalent of a shop), or log onto the *Web site* of an individual organization, or its distributor, and find information, prompt other contact or make a direct purchase electronically. While the methods may be changing consumer expectations of convenience, good service and value remain and must be dealt with much as they would be in doing business through any other channel.

KEY CONCEPTS AND THINKERS

By its nature distribution and channel management is enmeshed in the general process and literature of marketing. All the major commentators - and gurus if that is a better description for people like Philip

Kotler – have something sensible to say about it, though there is little that is outstanding or notably different, certainly as one body of ideas or information that stands out for recommendation. Everything must be distributed – products and services, consumer goods and everything involved in industrial and business to business marketing – so ideas about distribution and channel management are incorporated within those presented with a specific focus of this sort.

All this is perhaps unsurprising given the scope of the subject. It literally ranges across the whole marketing canvas and, especially these days, you are as likely to find useful ideas by checking under *e-commerce* as under specific distributive headings. However, a number of specialist books and others with good coverage of this area exist (and are listed in Chapter 9).

Here a small number of useful concepts likely to assist good channel management are explored. A simple one first offers a way of approaching channel choice.

Analyzing channel options

A useful approach to channel choice is described by F Bradley. In *International Marketing Strategy,* Prentice Hall, he says that: "In deciding a distribution strategy for international markets or in assessing existing channels the firm must consider the cost of the alternative chosen, the barriers to entry in the market, the orientation of intermediaries, the ability of the channel to distribute the range of the firm's products and the characteristics of the product or service and the customer." He uses a very effective framework to analyze this situation, based on what he calls the "Five C's." This framework is shown below (Table 8.1) and "allows the firm to establish its strategic goals with respect to channel management."

Like all such devices this is most useful simply as a guide to analysis and to help formalize thinking. Next another idea which is essentially simple is one of the most useful concepts in this area.

Market maps

The nature of distributive chains and arrangements lends itself to creating diagrams and flowcharts, indeed where this originated is anyone's guess. The concept here formalizes such approaches into

Table 8.1

Analyzing channels of distribution: the five C's framework

Coverage	Ability of channel to reach targeted customers to achieve market share and growth objectives
Character	Compatibility of channel with the firm's desired product positioning
Continuity	Loyalty of channel to the firm
Control	Ability of the firm to control total marketing program for the product or service
Cost	Investment required to establish and maintain the channel – variable associated with sales level. Fixed costs required to manage the channel: inventories, facilities, and training of sales force

specific form. To the best of my knowledge the term *market map* or *market system map* was originated by Michael T Wilson in his book *The Management of Marketing* (Gower Publishing); although this was published some time ago (1989 was the last edition) it remains a valuable text. The map aids analysis, planning and implementation, it describes the nature of the system, shows all the channels in existence or use and can be quantified to show what is happening where.

A simple example of a map, showing the various channels involved in the book publishing industry is shown below.

Preparing a map means:

1. listing the categories of consumers or end-users, and any subdivisions they may contain;
2. listing also any additional influencers (e.g. people having the role that architects do in specifying building materials); and
3. asking questions about customers and their characteristics so that information is clear alongside how their purchasing relates to the map, for example:

   » who are they? (e.g. male/female, age, buying power etc. for individuals and comparable information for industrial buyers – type of industry etc.);

» what are their needs? (e.g. for value, performance, convenience etc. – such factors can be linked specifically to a particular product);
» how are their needs being satisfied? (by both direct and, if relevant, indirect competition); and
» where do they buy? (linking to the different channels featured on the map).

This process may necessitate assembling significant amounts of data and ensuring that sales figures can be produced accurately in the right form, even some research may be useful. So be it. The detail is worth assembling and, with the right set up – for example computer programs that will link conventional sales data into "channel form" – much of it can be regularly updated very easily. Given the information, and a map to illustrate what is happening, there are several benefits stemming from the approach, it:

» assists planning and setting strategy (which channels to use/not use);
» monitors performance, allowing action to be taken to fine tune marketing action directed at specific channels;
» highlights the relationships involved (which customers use which channels etc.); and
» allows a view to be taken of matters such as pricing and profitability that reflects what is happening, not in an overall sense, but in the way individual channels work.

It is a concept upon which various tunes can be played, and which can assist in a variety of ways. The following example, shows just one aspect of this, and illustrates how reviewing channels can lead to fundamental changes in marketing approach.

Returning to the book market map, shown earlier (Figure 8.1), consider just two aspects of this: first books sold to traditional retailers, where the criteria for buying are well known. They vary by category of book, of course. Academic books say, may be judged in terms of their price, up to date nature, link with particular courses (a book officially recommended by a university is more likely to be bought and stocked than one just rated as "useful"), accessibility etc. and by the reputation, standing and presentation of the publisher (and author), and more. Buyers will tend to have common views and what needs to

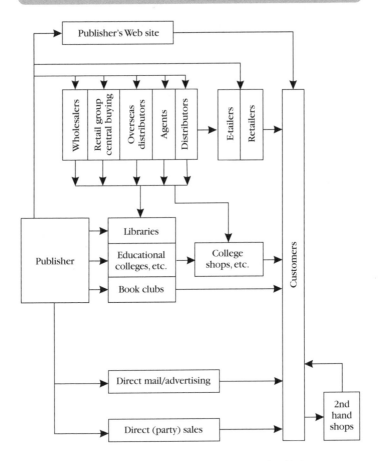

Fig. 8.1 System map showing channels involved in book publishing.

be put over to them can be addressed by the field sales team without (great) problem.

Secondly consider universities. Their bookshops may have similar criteria. But their academics have a different perspective and need handling differently. Yet they can be approached to try to secure adoption – agreement that a book becomes recommended reading. Opening a channel to this category of recommendation may increase sales through two channels, university and college bookshops and larger bookshops with academic departments. The link with such people is however radically different from that with the typical bookshop buyer, albeit those who buy academic titles. It almost certainly needs a different sales approach, it may even need sales people with different characteristics. But it is a channel that can be identified, an approach can be tailored for it and the information coming from updated market map views can assist in identifying this sort of situation, and in monitoring progress.

It must always be born in mind that it is a dynamic situation which is being viewed in this way, hence the necessary resolve to review on an ongoing basis. Academics may respond to presentations and want briefings of a particular sort, but they are busy people – how will they utilize the Internet in their task of finding and assessing suitable texts for the courses they teach? And what response will that need?

Assessing sources of power

The point has already been made (see Chapter 6) that there is a balance of power involved in many distribution situations. Sophisticated approaches exist to measure the relationships inherent here, particularly that between service quality and the power relationship between suppliers and distributors in a channel. The best known instrument here is the SERVQUAL approach. This can be used to assess existing products (it is based on researching past experience so cannot predict). It can be investigated via various articles, and was first documented in "An empirical assessment of the SERVQUAL scale," *Journal of Business Research*, Babakus, E and Boller, GW (1992).

The more learned business journals investigate ways of studying the power and service relationships regularly. Another, more recent article typical of these approaches is "The bases of power in international channels," *International Marketing Review*, by Ugur Yavas, Department of Management and Marketing, East Tennessee State University. Such references are very much at the academic end of the literature (some might say in the worst sense of the word academic). This later article is a dozen pages long and the language demands, let us just say, careful reading. That said there may be food for thought here for some people, certainly the service provided to distributors, and by them to their customers, should not just be regarded as a cost – the balance here needs careful consideration, and everything that makes a channel work effectively is worth noting.

An offensive approach

Amongst recent marketing books one that stands out and offers especially good advice about practical, yet creative, approaches to marketing is *Even More Offensive Marketing* (Gower Publishing). Its author, Hugh Davidson, is Chairman of Oxford Corporate Consultants and a visiting Professor of Consumer Marketing at Cranfield University School of Management. The book completely updates and replaces his original twenty-five-year-old and seminal book *Offensive Marketing*. Although he has, I think, only written these two books, both are excellent and the latest certainly encapsulates his experience of many years of consulting, presenting a stimulating action guide to approaches that are likely to lead to success in competitive markets.

It is a book worth an overall recommendation, but here it is the approaches set out about "Offensive Channel Marketing" that are particularly relevant. First, the offensive marketing approach is encapsulated in five key principles, illustrated by the mnemonic POISE, these are:

» *profitable*: balancing in an appropriate way the firm's need for profit and the customer's need for value;
» *offensive*: actively aiming to be a market leader, take risks and force competitors to become followers;
» *integrated*: working in a culture that permeates the whole organization and creates commitment to marketing;
» *strategic*: creating strategies based on probing analysis; and
» *effectively executed*: strong and disciplined execution implemented on a daily basis.

In terms of channel management he defines six key principles of an offensive approach:

1. Establish clear channel requirements for your brand
2. Use quantified portfolio analysis to determine channel strategies

3. Align channel and marketing strategies
4. Find ways to increase influence over your channels
5. Tailor your products and services to channel needs
6. Seek to develop new channels.

Given the action plan approach of the book, the chapter concerned (it is Chapter 15) sets out approaches in three main stages:

1. Fundamentals of offensive channel marketing:

» the role of marketing channels
» types of channels
» channels serve consumers
» channels are segmented
» channels add value to brands
» who owns consumer, key to channel profit
» branders can own channels
» growing competition across channels
» business to business marketing skills are essential.

2. Key principles of offensive channel marketing:

» establish channel requirements clearly
» use portfolio analysis to determine channel priorities
» align market and channel plans
» exercise influence over channels
» tailor your offer to channel needs
» present brands consistently across channels
» develop new channels.

3. 7-step process of offensive channel marketing:

» review and analyze channels
» project the future
» prioritize channels
» develop long term channel plan
» align channel and market plans
» develop customer and account plans
» monitor results.

Amongst writings on the topic that are likely to prompt the right approach this must rank high.

Finally, simple observation is one of the most important things here, research what is written about distribution and channel management by all means, but watch what is actually happening in the market place - your market place - as the prime means of keeping up to date.

Resources

- » Overseas distribution
- » A final e-thought
- » Key books
- » Articles
- » Useful Websites

"Distribution channels resemble the hour hand of a clock. They are always moving, but each individual movement is so small as to be almost imperceptible. The cumulative effect over a number of years can, however, be massive. New approaches to distribution are often easier to develop than superior products, yet they can often lead to equally large breakthroughs in profit."

Hugh Davidson, author "Even more Offensive Marketing"

The first area reviewed here focuses on distributors (of all sorts) used in international marketing.

OVERSEAS DISTRIBUTION

In setting up operations and distribution arrangements overseas a wealth of information may be necessary – about the market, the territory and its nature and culture, how things operate and, not least, about how to locate, check out and appoint a suitable distributor.

Good information can be obtained from a number of agencies, some of which are country specific. These include:

» banks
» chambers of commerce, including those overseas
» Department of Trade and Industry and British Overseas Trade Board
» The Institute of Export
» European Commission offices
» embassies and high commissions
» small business advisory agencies
» trade associations
» export clubs.

A good starting point is the Overseas Trade Services office (of DTI) at 66–74 Victoria Street, London EC2A 4HB Tel: 0207 247 9812 (stating the country in which you want to set up arrangements). An alternative route is to utilize the services of a local consultant, someone who can provide information and advice, undertake work "on the ground" and "hold your hand" as you explore a market for the first time. There is no substitute for good local knowledge and experience and, while such people need checking out, they provide a very practical route to setting up in an overseas market (one such is Gary Lim – see Acknowledgements – who can provide access to South East Asian markets).

Note that areas of specific information, such as tariffs, may be needed with regard to overseas markets. In addition, a number of organizations are sources of information and reports on overseas markets, these include:

» Dunn & Bradstreet International, Holmers Farm Way, High Wycombe, Bucks (Tel: 01494-422000)
» Infocheck Ltd, Vinery Court, 50 Banner Street, London EC1Y 8QE (Tel: 0207 251 3800)
» C.C.N. Business Information Ltd, Abbey House, Abbeyfield Road, Lenton, Notts NG7 2SW (Tel: 01159- 863864)
» Euromonitor Publications Ltd, 60-61, Britton Street, London EC1M 5NA (0207 251 8024)
» Trade Research Publications, 2 Wycliffe Grove, Werrington, Peterborough, PE4 5DE (Tel: 01733 573975).

NOTE: it is worth noting that the appointment of an overseas distributor needs a clear agreement and this, in turn, needs to be recorded in a contract. Setting this up may sensibly need the services of a good commercial lawyer. To illustrate the complexity, some of the factors are shown below (see box).

CONTRACTS WITH OVERSEAS DISTRIBUTORS

The following are amongst the key issues that need addressing and specifying in contracts:

» the parties to the agreement;
» the period and territories involved (and whether there is a trial period);
» the products to be distributed;
» prices, discounts and terms (and accounting for all financial arrangements);
» financial payments to the distributor (commission rates on different sales arrangements on territory etc.);

» specific responsibilities:
  » payment, credit checks and debt collection
  » delivery and transportation
  » local promotion and sales
  » service, including after sales service.
» matters of confidentiality and disclosure;
» measurement of success (and details of any targets set etc.);
» how any disputes will be handled, any arbitration arrangements (and under which countries laws the whole matter will be conducted); and
» termination arrangements.

A FINAL E-THOUGHT

With an eye on change, and the continuing development of the Internet, it is worth keeping up with the changes going on. Whether you see this form of business as for you or not at this stage, make sure that you have first hand experience of Internet shopping. Look at a site in some detail. Take a simple, well-known example, like that of Amazon. Log on and note:

» the ease of use (excellent);
» sales messages amongst the text (there are many, but they are made to fit well with the pure information content);
» use of illustrations (useful, but not so much or so complicated as to slow downloading to much); and
» on second visits, the way it becomes personalized to your use, with recommendations and news that fit your established interests.

And read Robert Spector's excellent book *Amazon.com: Get big fast* (Random House Business Books) and/or *Business the amazon.com way* (Rebecca Saunders, Capstone Publishing). This is an excellent example to take, it is a leader and its attention to detail in making its chosen way of business work is considerable and impressive. As *Business Week* reported, "What Bezos understood before most people was that the ability of the Web to connect almost anyone with almost any product meant that he could do things that couldn't be done in the physical world – such as sell 3 million books in a single store." It may be worth an in depth study to appreciate just what people are doing with this new methodology – and how it works for customers. Additionally, pick a site that is close to your own area of business and see what others are doing with that.

KEY BOOKS

The following are books about different aspects of distribution and channel management:

Rosenbloom B, (1995). *Marketing Channels: A Management View*. Fifth Edition. The Dryden Press, USA.

Hines P, Lamming R, Jones D, Cousins P Rich N, (2000). *Value Stream Management: Strategy and Excellence in the Supply Chain*. Prentice Hall.

Horchover D, Singletone S, (1999). *Choosing and Using a Foreign Agent or Distributor*. Croner Publications.

Friedman L, Furey G, Timothy R, (1999). *Channel Advantage: Going to market with multiple sales channels to reach more customers, sell more products*, make more profit. Butterworth Heinemann.

Rolnicki K, (1998). Managing Channels of Distribution: The Marketing Executive's Complete Guide. American Marketing Association.

The following are general texts with a good chapters on aspects of distribution and channel management:

Bradley F, (1995). *International Marketing Strategy*. Second Edition. Prentice Hall International (UK) Ltd.

Branch A E, (1990). *Elements Of Export Marketing and Management*. Second Edition. Chapman and Hall, Great Britain.

Elvy H B, (1998) *Marketing*. Butterworth-Heinemann.

Hall D, Jones R, Raffo C, (1999). *Business Studies*. Second Edition. Causeway Press Limited, Lancashire UK.

Hanson W, (2000). *Principles Of Internet Marketing*. South-Western College Publishing. Thomson Learning, USA.

Kotler P, Armstrong G, Saunders J, Wong V, (1999). *Principles Of Marketing*, Second European Edition, Prentice Hall Europe

Kotler P, (2000). *Marketing Management*. International Edition. Prentice Hall International, Inc.

ARTICLES

Given the fact that the literature on the subject is small, it is worth keeping an eye on articles. All the main marketing journals – *Marketing, Marketing Week, Marketing Business, Sales and Marketing Management (USA), Journal of Business & Industrial Marketing, Journal of International Marketing, Revolution* etc. – touch on the subject from time to time. For those selling through retail channels there are journals, like *Retail Week,* that look at this aspect of the subject exclusively.

In addition there is information available on a variety of Internet sites, though again none are specific.

USEFUL WEBSITES

Because distribution and channel management is an integral part of marketing, the following, while they deal with marketing on a broad scale, specialize in research reports and may contain useful information:
www.keynote.co.uk
Reports from a variety of industries from a major market research firm.
www.verdict.co.uk
From a retail research specialist information here focuses on that sector.
www.datamonitor.co.uk
Provide off the peg or bespoke reports on the state of many different industries.
www.store.eiu.com
Part of the *Economist* group, the Economist Intelligence Unit has been a leader in industry analysis for many years.
www.mintel.com
Leading publisher of consumer product market data; 400 reports are issued every year.
www.eMarketer.com
Consolidated information from hundreds of leading research sources make this site a recognized authority on online marketing; their free

newsletter is a useful way to keep up to date with developments in this fast-changing area.

There is a profusion of such sites and it may be worth taking the view of overall bodies such as the marketing institutes, especially in major markets such as UK (the Chartered Institute of Marketing) and USA (American Marketing Association: www.ama.org) before selecting a number to investigate.

Ten Steps to Making Channel Management Work

» Making the selection
» Deciding the channel mix
» Ensuring a customer focus
» Managing the channels
» Influencing those involved along the channels
» Treat channels like markets
» Tailor products and services to channels
» Match marketing activity to individual channels
» Monitor channel performance
» Innovate and seek new solutions

"Business success is based ever more directly and speedily on the abilities of the people in business to change, foresee trends, take acceptable risks, be more in tune with tomorrow's needs of today's customers and to set their stalls out for the myriad economic and social changes which are occurring."

John Harvey-Jones, consultant, author and former Chairman of ICI Industries

As we have seen channel management consists essentially of taking a marketing approach to the area of distribution. Goods and services must be got to market, and there are many options available – many potential chains of distribution. Decisions about *what* to do are important, but so too is what is done to make distribution work and that too defines managing channels. In reviewing a complex process it is difficult to say "these are *the* ten things that make it work," so here let me say only that these are ten important things about making it work. It should not be taken as devaluing any other factor that these ten are in the spotlight; they do however cover the main points.

1. MAKING THE SELECTION

The first principle to recognize here is that there is a selection to make. Just because things are performing well does not mean that existing channels are right, much less that they will be right forever. There may be some routes you can rule out at once for obvious reasons, though even "obvious reasons" may sensibly be questioned and other routes all need consideration.

There are a number of factors to balance. These include:

» customers, and different customer types;
» product characteristics;
» distributor characteristics – literally what skills and resources do they "bring to the party";
» competition, and the question of copying, matching or avoiding what they do;
» your own organization, for example what is better done in-house? What is better left to a distributor? And

» overall economic and environmental factors affecting your product and markets.

Research and analysis may be necessary here and some options that may not seem so far apart (e.g. exclusive or non-exclusive dealers) may in fact have important differences that demand investigation to enable the right choice to be made.

Remember too that many options have legal consequences. If you sign an agreement with a particular distributor, say, then you may have to live with it; at least for a while. You do not want to run foul of a problem that simple checking could have prevented.

So, the key things here are to:

» review the options widely;
» gather the necessary information; and
» take time to study the options and the information you have about them.

The whole process may need to be repeated literally market by market if you operate internationally.

2. DECIDING THE CHANNEL MIX

The point has been made that channel choice is not a matter of picking *the* route to market; that is right for few organizations. It is a matter of picking a mix of channels that make sense and deciding the relative importance of each.

This is not simply a matter of ranking them. It means making decisions about your investment in each and forecasting what each will do for you.

The "market map" concept (see Chapter 8) helps clarify what may be a complex picture. It allows the total picture to be taken in, and the way one channel performs to be reviewed alongside others. Channel mix must reflect a clear strategy, that is a clear strategy for *each* channel. As different channels may be used for widely different purposes each (and every) one must be managed to achieve its own particular objectives.

EXAMPLE

A manufacturer of motor car tires can sell through two completely different channels. One aims to sell tires to the manufacturers of cars that need tires as original equipment. The other aims to sell car owners replacement tires. The two are clearly different and also clearly need different approaches, one to access the comparatively small number of motor manufacturers, the other the numerous and different kinds of outlet selling replacement tires (from garages to specialist tire centers).

Deciding the mix means making decisions about which channels to use for what (and which not to use), about how to maximize the effectiveness of each channel and about priorities between the number of different routes involved.

3. ENSURING A CUSTOMER FOCUS

Choice of channels is not just a matter of convenience or of finance (or indeed of convention). Channels are there to facilitate the process of purchase. If customers do not like something then, especially in an age of choice, they will vote with their feet as it were. And this principle is certainly true of channels. Distribution links to the four P's of marketing; the fourth is usually defined as place. But there is more than just location to worry about here.

» *Location*: this is, of course important: does the customer want to buy at home, in the high street, at an out-of-town shopping center? Or somewhere else? (e.g. on the Internet). The answer may well be that different customers want different things and that channel organization must accommodate their wishes if it is to maximize sales.

» *Location "plus"*: this separate heading makes the point that there is more to a location than just where it is. A high street may seem convenient, but how close is parking? Travel to the place of purchase is a major factor in customer choice, which is especially fickle about such things. In the nearest small town to my home, even the far end of the high street is regarded as less accessible than its core area (and parking is pretty good).

» *Service*: this is important too. Some products need a degree of advice and information to assist their purchase, and all benefit from service in the pure "good customer contact sense." If your product needs advice before people will choose and buy then the chosen channel must be able to provide it. Again here are compromises to be made here – but customers will decide what's best for them, and may well have the option of deciding that your product is just too complicated to buy and move on to a competitor that has things better organized.

Although it is right to use the word compromise in so complex a setting, customer satisfaction is clearly vital and everything else must take account of that.

4. MANAGING THE CHANNELS

This heading separates the need to manage the channel mix in an organizational sense from the separate need to influence people along the routes (see point 5 next). Managing the channels in this sense means:

» incorporating specific channel focused activity into the marketing plan;
» setting clear priorities for making each channel work;
» allocating people appropriately (for example, who will be accountable for the customers in different channels and how will these customers be serviced – remember the differences inherent in the car tire example earlier; and
» creating and maintaining appropriate service back up for each channel (and for each kind of customer, including the ultimate customer).

It also includes matching a whole range of activities to the nature of particular channels and customers. For example, transport and distribution need to be equipped with trucks the size of which relates to the deliveries that need to be made to particular kinds of customer. Change this and the fleet may be rendered obsolete.

5. INFLUENCING THOSE INVOLVED ALONG THE CHANNELS

This is certainly one of the most important areas to consider. You have to sell to customers, and create, maintain and develop relationships with them; this links to another topic beyond our brief here but worth mentioning, that of account management.

In addition, you may well need to:

» *Inform* them about the product, your plans, how things are going, opportunities to come – and more. An ongoing dialogue is necessary here;
» *Motivate* them, especially if contact is infrequent or difficult, as with overseas distributors; and
» *Support* them, with for example joint promotions, merchandising or advice, training – anything they expect or find useful.

This ongoing communication may use every available method, from simple e-mail to video conferencing, and must be planned and sustained (and therefore budgeted for in both time and money). It is all too easy to think that just because your product sells well, a contract exists, your advertising is good or whatever, people will complete the role you hope for with regard to selling on the product unbidden, as it were.

Success in managing channels effectively is down in large measure to this sort of communications program; it should have clear objectives, be systematically undertaken and creatively executed.

6. TREAT CHANNELS LIKE MARKETS

In all respects this is an important one. Markets vary. They are dynamic and can be fast changing. The people in different markets see things differently and expect their viewpoints to be understood and respected by their suppliers.

All activity needs to be tailored to individual channels. This is easier when channels are very different (as in the earlier car tire example), but needs more conscious thought when differences are less obvious.

7. TAILOR PRODUCTS AND SERVICE TO CHANNELS

A well-known brand of chocolate may be an international brand, and it may well appear essentially the same in Bangkok, Boston, and Brussels. In all likelihood it is not. To take just one factor as an example, the product must have a higher melting point when sold in hot countries. Now it might be made possible to sell the standard version in a hot part of the world (it could be transported in refrigerated containers). But it must also survive local distribution, and it might well be that no one will handle it unless it does so – after all, the local distributor will get the complaints.

This is an obvious example perhaps, but it does show how everything must relate to the market and thus to the channel. Instructions are necessary if furniture is to be sold through some channels in flat-pack form. Packaging (or boxes) might contain more information for technical products sold through channels where the outlets can or do provide less advice and information than others, as might instructions (and both will need translating for overseas markets).

Thus an important part of the decision making and management relating to channels is about fitting products to channels, rather than simply fitting channels to (existing) products. More complication, yes, but it helps get a fit which works effectively.

8. MATCH MARKETING ACTIVITY TO INDIVIDUAL CHANNELS

This needs comment in terms of marketing at various levels. Let us take advertising as an example. It may need to:

» incorporate channel information to make it clear how something can be purchased; and
» be directed not only at the ultimate consumer but at intermediaries along the distributive chain.

And it should always be appropriate and well directed to its target audience. Different strategies are involved here. Some international brands use the same advertising world-wide (e.g. Coca Cola), others will focus on different markets in different ways.

This kind of link has to be born in mind whatever the product. Having settled on a strategy then its implications must be worked out. Look, for example, at the difference in advertising in the computer area between Dell who sell direct and whose ads target potential purchasers, corporate or not, in a similar way, and other companies who need a response that takes people into a dealership that may well sell competing brands. The latter want people to walk in already feeling strongly that their brand is right, and perhaps with a pre-conditioned *accept no substitutes* frame of mind.

The range of circumstances here is immense, but the principle is clear. Everything along one chain, may differ from everything else along another and all marketing activity must be designed to work in the knowledge that that is so and of what those differences are.

9. MONITOR CHANNEL PERFORMANCE

A channel is not for life. The dynamic situations inherent here have been mentioned more than once. Given that what is being implemented is a mix, it is a prime part of channel management to monitor performance. To be more specific – to monitor comparative performance of all channels in order to:

» improve the way an individual channel performs;
» better balance the mix, putting more emphasis on one channel and reducing it on another, perhaps; and
» ultimately, perhaps, to change radically the way distribution is handled.

The quick and easy way to review this is with the "market map" concept (an excellent tool that can be used either as a broad brush or to produce more precise information – see Chapter 8). More sophisticated techniques are also available.

For whatever reasons, the overall aspects of channel selection and management seem to remain unreviewed longer than many other aspects of marketing. This is both likely to leave you open to danger and to risk missing opportunities. Review should be a prescribed and structured process.

10. INNOVATE AND SEEK NEW SOLUTIONS

Finally, as part of the ongoing regular review mentioned above, new developments should be observed and new options sought (after all *someone* has to be first with some things – why not you?).

Let us be clear what we mean here by "new." It would be entering new territory to organize party plan selling for a product never sold that way before, but it would not be *new* – the technique has been tried and tested elsewhere. But it could well create a new mix of channels used and that, in turn, might produce increased sales.

Sometimes there is significant innovation that affects many organizations. This may be something like a move to out of town shopping centers, or something technologically led like the whole area of IT and e-commerce. In practice many innovations are seemingly minor changes – evolution is more common than revolution – but that does not mean that they are not worthwhile. They may well be, and a series of them may be still more useful.

At the end of the day what makes channel management successful is much the same as makes any aspect of marketing successful. It needs to be:

» *customer focused*: because ultimately, however innovative, however clever something is the final arbiter is in the market place;
» *continuous*: in its implementation and in its review, because ongoing refinement and improvement should be inherent in a dynamic marketplace;
» *co-ordinated*: because a complex mix is involved and one aspect of it may well affect all the others; and
» *creative*: because what matters is what works and preferably what works better than whatever it is competitors are doing, not what the rule book says.

If the principles of good channel management are well applied, then it has the potential to positively contribute to the marketing process and, in so doing, to help provide a positive edge in the market.

Frequently Asked Questions (FAQs)

Q1: What does channel management encompass?

A: Chapter 1 defines the process and puts it in context.

Q2: Why is channel management important?

A: Chapter 3 shows how its importance has increased over time.

Q3: What are the criteria for selecting the right distributors?

A: Chapter 6 describes the role of distributors and suggests what makes for good ones.

Q4: Must distribution be differently organized when overseas markets are involved?

A: There are certainly special issues to be born in mind here, Chapter 5 explains.

Q5: How frequently should I contact distributors?

A: Chapter 6 investigates the vital area of communication with distributors – why it should be done, how it should be done and how often.

Q6: How is e-commerce changing channel mix?

A: Chapter 4 investigates the overall impact of the IT revolution

Q7: There is so much involved, what exactly needs to be done?

A: Chapter 7 gives a variety of examples of good practice, illustrating different aspects of channel management.

Q8: How can I be sure my channel mix is working well?

A: Chapter 10 summarizes the key factors involved in making the process work.

Q9: How do I find out more about the subject?

A: Chapter 9 – Resources.

Q10: Will distributive options and practice continue to change?

A: Chapter 7 touches on the future, Chapter 7 makes clear the dynamic nature of the process.

Acknowledgments

I can claim no credit for the origination of the unique format of the series of which this work is part. So thanks are due to those at Capstone who did so, and for the opportunity they provided for me to play a small part in so significant and novel a publishing project.

I am grateful to Gary Lim, of Gary Lim Associates in Singapore, for providing case material from Asia; he is always as helpful as he is hospitable when I visit his home city. Last, but by no means least, thanks to Emily Smith who acted as researcher searching out back-up material and references that saved me time and helped me meet a tight deadline. She took on the task at short notice and did a thoughtful, thorough and useful job; such help is much appreciated.

Patrick Forsyth
Touchstone Training & Consultancy
28 Saltcote Maltings
Maldon
Essex CM9 4QP

Acknowledgments

Index